HOW THE

·DEVIL·

BECAME

PRESIDENT

EUGENE SHAPIRO

PIR○PRESS

PirOPress
Kenwood, CA
www.HowTheDevilBecamePresident.com
DavidSavage4President@hotmail.com

Publisher's Note: This is a work of fiction. Names, characters, places, and incidents are a product of the author's imagination. Locales and public names are sometimes used for atmospheric purposes. Any resemblance to actual people, living or dead, or to businesses, companies, events, institutions, or locales is completely coincidental.

Book production: AuthorFriendly.com

How the Devil Became President of the United States / Eugene Shapiro—1st ed.

978-0-9677496-4-8 print
978-0-9677496-3-1 digital

"The Devil frequently fills our thoughts with great schemes."
—St. Teresa of Avila, Interior Castle

"Finally, an honest politician who admits being the Devil."
—Raymond Foxglove, Anchor/Host, The Missing Point, TCN-TV

"We have never heard the Devil's side of the story,
God wrote all the books."
—Anatole France

Dedicated to the one and only one.

Greetings:

I am David Savage. I am running for President of the United States in 2016. I have asked Eugene Shapiro to write the way I shall run my campaign. I have dictated each and every word to Eugene and he has diligently and accurately put them into a readable form. I very much appreciate his enterprise and he will be rewarded when the time comes.

In the meantime, I hope that each and every one of you enjoys my story and vote when the time comes.

In sickness and in health,

David Savage

PROLOGUE

Allow me to introduce myself: I am David Savage. I am the Devil and I am running for President of the United States. I've taken the name David Savage in my current incarnation. I am a much-ballyhooed celebrity and real estate developer. I have changed many neighborhoods to make way for my luxury towers. Some would say I am a destroyer, but few would say that to my face. People are always jealous of success. And, to be sure, I am very successful—always have been, always will be. I live in New York City, in a penthouse in a pre-war building on Upper Fifth Avenue. People ask me why I don't live in one of my high-rise luxury buildings: Savage Towers, Savage East Side Tower, Savage International Hotel and Tower, or Savage World Towers? To tell the truth, they are all too modern for me. As you will see, I am nostalgic for things of the past.

A little about myself: I am tall with an athletic build, a chiseled clean-shaven face, a sharp nose, and penetrating—if I may say so myself—dazzling metallic green eyes. I've appeared on the cover of many magazines, and *Time Magazine* even referred to me as candy for the eyes. I like that term…and it does suit me.

My hair is pitch black, slicked, long in the back and just nibbling at my shirt collar. As old as I am, I still walk like a young man, body erect, eyes focused in front, determined to capture the future.

My clothes are always impeccable, as if I had just stepped out of *Gentleman's Quarterly*. In fact, *GQ* featured me in its last issue. My uniform is a handmade Italian pinstripe suit, white shirt, Hermes tie, and soft Italian loafers. And… of course, there is my signature piece: a silk flora handkerchief in my breast pocket.

My adversary in this episode, titled *How the Devil Became President*, is Abe Kandinsky. Abe is a dear friend of mine, perhaps my only friend. Abe owns Kandinsky's Upper West Side Delicatessen—Kosher since 5720. The deli is on Broadway near 88th street. Abe lives alone in a floor-through apartment above the deli. The deli and the apartments are in a five-story tenement walk-up building he owns.

Abe's craggy face, balding-on-top white hair, and short white beard give him the look of a man of 65, although, like me, he is much, much older. His brow has wrinkle lines stretching from ear to ear, as if he spends all his time worrying. (Between you and me, Abe does worry too much. You see, he always expects everything to turn out just right—perfect—but as with all of life, it never does.) Abe also sprouts numerous spider lines running from the edges of both eyes into his cheeks. His basset-like, melancholy, deep-set brown eyes are always open, as opposed to mine, and inviting. Mine are inviting, but in a different way.

Abe's a big man: wide shoulders, broad chest, and muscular arms. With his broken nose, he could easily be mistaken for an ex-heavyweight boxer. He walks with a labored gait. For some reason, unknown to me, he has invited arthritis to creep into his joints. And his posture sucks: always walking with his neck and head bent down as if he is looking out for dog poop, or a more universal explanation, carrying the weight of the world on his shoulders.

Okay! So, that's us. But I should go back to the beginning, actually before the beginning.

In the beginning darkness covered all. Out of the darkness came the Earth. And the Earth was divided between the waters and the dry land. The dry land brought forth herb-yielding seeds, fruit trees, and grass. Out of the seas rose the great whales and living creatures that moved in the waters. On the dry land came the creeping things and all kinds of beasts. And all the living things lived peacefully in the waters and peacefully on the dry land.

God saw what He had done and declared: "This is Good!"

"What good?" I cried. I wasn't known as the Devil yet. I was standing beside God and had witnessed the creation. "They need to do what they are!" I announced.

No sooner had I said that, and the animals on the dry land began devouring one another. In the waters, the big fish began to eat the little fish.

"What are you doing?" God demanded, scratching his head in disbelief.

"I'm helping them discover their true being—their inner animal."

"Can't you leave well enough alone?" God's frustration echoed through the universe. He always made a lot of noise, rumblings, lightning, big waves, floods, hurricanes. He eventually became known as the Creator, but he was equally good at destroying. Although, I must say, he rarely was assigned the blame. That always went to me. "Jeez," God said, "you are a pain!"

"Why are you kvetching?" I asked him.

"Look." God spoke to me as if to an annoying child. That's what he always thought of me. He wasn't Abe Kandinsky then. That would take a long time to develop.

"I've been busy for six straight days." He voice was like thunder rolling over the hills. "I'm tired. I want to rest."

I laughed at his whining. "You sound like an old Jew."

"I am an old Jew." God tugged at his long, white beard. "I'm tired because you keep causing trouble with my creation."

While we were talking, a new creature appeared on dry land.

"What's that?" I asked.

"That, my dear brother, is man." God was himself again, smiling, content, and secure in his own omnipotence. "Now I can rest. You won't be able to mess with him."

Oh, yeah, I thought to myself, my eyes glinting behind half-closed lids.

"I created him in my image," God proudly announced. "He's perfect!"

"Perfect, huh? Wanna Bet?" I challenged.

And so began the history of the world. God and I are always on Earth as human beings, always a part of the action, manipulating events. And we bet. For example: would Moses cross the Red Sea, would Caesar survive the Ides of March, would Joan free France, would Elizabeth defeat the Spanish Armada, would the Americans beat the British, would Lindbergh cross the Atlantic, would the Red Sox win the World Series two years in a row?

That's what we do. God and I. We bet.

You have to understand that the Earth is simply a test…a game for us to play in. God, because He created Man in his image, always bets that Man will do the right thing. I, on the other hand, knowing the real nature of Man, always bet Man will look for the easy solutions and be ready to sell out.

Now you're up to date. In the summer of 2016, we showed up in New York City, Manhattan to be exact. We decided what we wanted to be, and it was as if we had always been there.

1

Abe and I love baseball. We'd been fans from the beginning. Abe—he was then known as Billy Cavendish—codified the rules as a member of the New York Knickerbocker Club in 1854. Cavendish was sure the game would become the "National Pastime," a phrase he coined. I doubted it. "Wanna Bet?" Cavendish asked. Of course I bet. He won that one.

So in the fall of 2016, Abe and I were standing at the urinals in Yankee Stadium when a drunken fan, talking loudly on his cell phone, came weaving in, tottering toward us.

Without turning around, I raised my left hand and swatted it backwards.

The fool felt the blow and fell into a toilet cubicle. Trying not to fall, he reached out to hold onto the door and dropped his cell phone into the toilet bowl. He reached in to retrieve it. He wasn't quick enough. I had already flushed it.

"That wasn't nice," Abe said to me.

I didn't answer. I was listening to the game being broadcast into the room. "This is the bottom of the ninth, two on, runners at second and third, and the Yankees are down by one. Rodriguez is behind in the count, one ball, two strikes."

"It's over," Abe smirked; sure he was going to win the bet. His money was always on the Yankees.

I, on the other hand, always bet against the Yankees. It was my perverse counterintuitive response, as I too always wore pinstripes.

"You're gonn'a lose this time, boychick," Abe said, buttoning his fly. "He's gonn'a bring 'em in."

"Wanna bet he strikes out?"

"Strike out!" Abe stepped away from the urinal. "What? The guy's hitting 437 with runners in scoring position."

"Don't be so naïve. This was his contract year. He signed for one hundred twenty million."

"So?" Abe looked down at his hands as he washed them. They were the hands of a man who had worked hard all his life.

"So, he got his money and doesn't care anymore," I said.

"You're so damn cynical," Abe stammered. He always stammered a little when he got excited. "I just don't understand you."

"What's there to understand?" I joined Abe at the washbasin, but didn't wash my hands. First of all, I had gotten a manicure that afternoon and didn't want to spoil the polish. And besides, my dick wasn't dirty. "The difference between us is that I understand human nature."

"Right! And I don't?"

"No, you don't!" I snarled at him. "You are so naive. You keep expecting them to be good, to do the right thing."

"What's wrong with that? I made them in my image."

"Ah! Oh! Your image. It wasn't a real image. It was an image of what you imagined to be your image."

"You're just jealous because you came after me."

"No, I'm not jealous. We're twins and you just happened to come out first... and not by much."

"Enough to make a difference—"

The announcer's voice filled the room. "Rodriguez steps out of the batter's box. Takes a few swings. Now, he's back."

"Watch this," I said to Abe.

"Here's the pitch." The announcer's excited, expectant voice flooded the room. "Rodriguez swings. Oh, MY GOD! He swung at a terrible pitch and struck out."

Groans could be heard throughout the stadium.

With a wide smile on my face, I took Abe's arm to escort him out of the men's room.

Abe removed my hand and said, "Now you watch this."

Out on the field, the ball Rodriguez missed fell out of the catcher's mitt. It rolled under his feet toward the stands. The runner from third came roaring in to score. The catcher retrieved the ball. He threw it to third to catch the runner coming in from second. The ball went over the third baseman's head. The runner scored, winning the game for the Yankees.

2

Abe and I left the stadium with the crowd. We slowly walked toward a sports bar across 161st street.

We hadn't spoken since we had left the men's room. Abe had grabbed a hot dog from a stand that was closing down and was munching on it as we crossed the street. Once Abe finished the hot dog, I spun him around. "Damn it! He struck out. Why couldn't you leave it at that? No, not you. You always have to fix things your way."

Abe looked down at my hand on his arm. He wasn't much of a feely, touchy guy, so I removed my hand. He spread his arms apart. "I wouldn't have to fix things if you didn't mess around."

"Me!" I exclaimed, as innocently as possible. "I don't mess anything. I simply bet that this man you created in your image is not all that perfect."

"Oh, not perfect, boubbily. If you left him alone, he would figure it out."

"Really? Like who?"

"Job," was Abe's immediate response.

"Well," I had to admit, "you won that bet. But I'll win the next one about your wonderful man."

"Oh, really mister big-shot billionaire developer. Do you think people will let you get away with tearing down another building?"

"Here's what you don't understand, mister mensch." I jabbed a finger into Abe's chest. "Americans like the rich. And you know why?"

"No. I know nothing," Abe answered, shaking his head from side to side, playing the victim. "You tell me."

"Everyone in America believes they can be rich." I couldn't help grinning from ear to ear.

"And why's that?" Abe stammered.

"Because they're fools. They all expect to make it to the top one percent. So they let the rich do whatever they want. Schmucks! Believing that when they get rich they can do whatever they want."

Abe's response when he had no argument was always the same. Fight it out. He put two fists in front of him, ready to box. "You're a real piece of work," he said as he threw a jab at me.

I feigned to the left.

"You think you can throw hard-working people and the poor out on the street?" He threw a jab at my middle. I stepped back.

He then threw a right that landed softly on my jaw. It didn't matter. He couldn't hurt me even if he meant it.

He wasn't done yet: "You think you can build yet another unnecessary high-rise luxury building for the super rich?"

I went cold and let out a deep guttural howl that would have frozen any mortal in his tracks. Of course, it had no effect on Abe. So I switched gears and pinched both of his cheeks. "And you my dear brother, think that by being one of the working stiffs and helping poor people, you can make them happy."

I took his arm and we walked into the sports bar.

3

Casey's Sports Bar had occupied the corner of 161st and River Avenue since 1924. The bar was a long tunnel of a room, a teak bar running most of its length, with wooden stools and hanging light fixtures dating back to when it opened. The room was no more than 35-feet wide, so everyone was essentially in everyone else's face.

By the time we walked in, the bar was packed with rowdy fans extending their drunken celebration of the Yankees' miraculous victory. I loved the smell of the place: testosterone mingling with spilt beer.

As we pushed our way toward the bar, I turned to Abe. "My people... less than perfect."

I shook hands with every man we passed as we moved toward the back of the room. There were no women in the bar. No one ever expected any woman to come. I slapped the backs of several men exclaiming, "Great game. Great game." They all high-fived me back.

I stared at two men in front of us standing at the bar. Within seconds they walked away, making room for Abe and me.

Gus, the bartender, a grizzled, tattooed, unshaven man in his late fifties came across the bar from us. He eyed us with disdain. *Who de fuck was des two? Some fucking dude in a fucking suit and a fucking Jew with his little hat.*

(I should mention that when he was in the mood, Abe wore a black yarmulke on the top of his head. It was his "statement." In spite of his chaotic history with his chosen people, he was always ready to defend his Jewishness.)

Gus didn't say a word or nod his head in greeting. He just stared at us.

I loved this guy! "Good evening," I pleasantly said. "I'll have a Gray Goose martini, up with a twist and two olives—olives with pimentos, please."

"What's *pementoes*?" Gus asked, knowing full well what they were, yet mispronouncing the word. "We only have olives."

"You mean green olives?" I asked politely.

"Yeh," Gus spit out the word, staring hard at me.

I smiled at the bartender and said, "Well, why don't you go take a look at your olives, and maybe you'll find two with *pementoes*. They're probably buried at the bottom of the jar."

"And you?" Gus snarled, turning to Abe. The only thing missing from his question was the word *kike*.

"Just a tonic with very little ice. I presume you do have ice?"

Gus glared at Abe for a moment and then walked away.

Abe called after him. "Make that a diet tonic, if you have one."

That done we turned our attention to the TV monitors showing the highlights of the game we had just seen.

"Ah," Abe said gesturing to me. "Maybe I should have used instant replay when I started."

I chose to ignore him and pointed a finger at the TV. All the monitors changed to TCN, a cable news show discussing the race for the Presidential nominations.

That brought an instant jeer of boos from the crowd.

"Come on, David," Abe said. "Give them what they want."

"That, my dear Abe," I replied, "is what I do, what I always do. I don't deny them anything... not like you."

The bartender tried to change the channel on the TVs. Nothing worked. "Something's wrong with the reception. It's frozen," Gus yelled out.

That brought a sustained round of boos.

Gus threw his hands up in the air. "Sorry guys. It must be the fucking cable," he said and went back to making our drinks.

What he found surprised him. All the olives had pimentos in them. He reached down into a refrigerator under the counter to get another jar. "Fuck," he muttered to himself. There were two unopened jars and both had olives with pimentos. He couldn't believe it. He never ordered anything but plain olives.

On the TV monitors were the well-known and once highly respected anchor/commentator, Raymond Foxglove. His white beard and mustache were carefully trimmed to give credence to his self-proclaimed adventurous conservatism. He was wearing a black suit, plain shirt, and nondescript tie. He was standing alone in the center of a large, technologically equipped studio, holding onto his clipboard. The name of the program—*The Missing Point*—ran along the bottom of the screen. The monitor had a live picture of Abel Carran holding onto the railing of a set of stairs leading up to his G5 private jet.

4

Carran was expected to be a shoe-in for the Republican nomination. It was a month before the convention and he was polling in the high sixties. He was running on the fact that he had been, or rather *was*, a successful businessman and knew how to make things work.

It worked for him, his family, and his stockholders. The layoffs and moving his corporate and manufacturing headquarters to the Far East did wonders for the bottom line. It didn't work for his employees, their families, and the communities where they lived.

Carran was in his sixties, tall, baby-faced, with carefully sculpted unruly hair and a squeaky speaking voice. He was a glad-hander with a tight little smile. He always played himself up as an "average guy." The fact that he was worth 150 million belied his common-man image.

Carran had been a quarterback in college. Never made it to the pros. He married Nancy Hubbard, a woman whose father had a chicken factory in Georgia. He went to work for his father-in-law and came up with the idea of micro-specialization: forget whole chickens. Just do wings; ten different varieties of frozen chicken wings. They wholesaled the whole (sans wings) chickens and shipped the wings all over America. Carran's father-in-law made a fortune.

Carran too. Once he made his first 25 million, he left his father-in-law's business and started his own competing company. He moved to China and never had to worry about whole chickens. He just bought wings. He never thought or cared about what the Chinese did with the chickens. He took all the wings they could supply, created his sauce variations, froze the wings in specially designed refrigerated containers, and shipped them all over the world.

He dabbled in real estate, put some money into venture capital, bought a house in the Cayman Islands, and divorced his wife. Many people called him callous, as he no longer needed her father's money. Carran insisted the divorce came about after he had fallen in love with another woman. He always left out the part that she was a much younger woman. He had been involved with her for years while he was still married. Eventually, he married her. As far as he was concerned, that proved how much he loved her.

Not quite enough, however, as he continued to have affairs outside of that marriage and the marriage that followed. He had brushed his marital history under the carpet and was campaigning as America's conservative champion.

"Good Evening Ambassador," Foxglove said when he knew he was live. Carran had spent a little over a year as the U.S. Ambassador to Honduras and demanded all call him by that title.

"Mr. Ambassador," Foxglove said flashing his broad grin, lots-of-white-teeth signature smile. "We understand you have challenged all candidates to sign the Family Vow."

Carran took his hand off the railing and leaned forward toward the camera. He almost lost his balance, but caught hold of the railing and held on. "That's correct, Ray. I signed it and I think anyone running in this Christian country should be required to sign. Both parties—left or right."

"Then you are asking Governor Dickey to sign it? Is that correct?" The camera stayed on Carran as Foxglove talked.

"Well," Carran spread his hands apart, "whoever is running for President."

"Right now," Foxglove fired back, "that would be Governor Dickey."

"Whoever," was Carran's short quip.

"You don't think your marriage history flies in the face of the Family Vow?"

"Look!" Carran's eyes went hard and his face flushed. "Look, I have made mistakes in the past. Who hasn't? Now I see clearer and believe the Family Vow will take America back to her Christian roots." He paused. The camera stayed on him. He took several steps up the stairs toward the open jet door, turned, and said, "In fact, I'm for an amendment to the Constitution." Carran forced a smile and continued, "Thank you." He went up the stairs and disappeared into the jet.

One of the men at Casey's Sports Bar shouted, "Fuck you!"

Another shouted, "Asshole!" That was enough to get the men at the bar, who were already several sheets to the wind, to start throwing straws, lemon wedges, and peanuts at the TV monitors.

"Com'on Gus," someone shouted, "get this fuck off."

Gus raised his hands in surrender. "Not my fault guys. It's fucking stuck."

Carran came back out of the jet. He came down the stairs and stood in front of the camera. "Look... forgiveness is a great part of the American and Christian traditions." Again, the forced smile. He waved three fingers of his right hand in the air and offered, "God, country, traditional marriage, and the sanctity of the fetus."

That would become his campaign slogan. It had just come bubbling out of his mouth. He turned, and started up the stairs to the jet.

5

The crowd in Casey's Sports Bar knew what to do with Carran's slogan. One started singing, "My fetus tis of thee..."

"Fetus, fetus," another roared. "Has anyone seen my fetus?"

Then the straws and peanuts started flying as the boos grew louder. It was so nuts in there. I was laughing my head off. I turned to Abe and pointed a finger at the disappeared Carran. "There's your perfect man, Abe. He opens his mouth, using words and saying nothing. Remember what Plato said?" I asked Abe.

"He said a lot of things."

"I'm thinking of democracy."

"What about democracy?"

"He said it would eventually wind up as chaos."

Gus brought our drinks. He glared at me. "I can't find any permentoes." He had gouged the pimentos out of the olives. He also made sure to splash some of the martini on the bar when he set the glass down in front of me. I loved this guy.

He placed Abe's tonic on the bar.

"Thank you," Abe said, trying not to laugh.

The TV monitors showed Foxglove in the TCN studio. "We also have Governor Dickey, the Democrat frontrunner on a satellite hookup."

The screen switched to a street scene outside the Four Seasons Restaurant in Manhattan where Harriet Dickey, the Governor of New York, dressed in a robin blue pantsuit, was standing in front of a microphone.

Dickey had gone from Yale Law School to a U.S. Senate staffer, to New York legislator, to a member of the House of Representatives, to Governor of New York. She had blazed a trail to get where she was, leaving lots of corpses in her wake.

Her appearance brought immediate taunts and boos from the crowd at the bar. Peanuts were thrown at the TV monitors.

Foxglove's voice came over the TV. "Governor Dickey, what do you think of Mr. Carran's challenge for you to sign the Family Vow?"

Dickey smiled. It wasn't a beautiful smile: too studied and self-conscious. "Well, first of all, I don't think anyone should campaign for or against the fetus until they have carried one."

"Go get 'em, girl," someone at the bar yelled, and the crowd broke into a cheer.

Foxglove decided to stay away from that one. "What about a Constitutional Amendment for traditional marriages?"

"I'm sure Abel Carran knows what's right for him, but I don't need an amendment to the Constitution to define marriage. I've been married for thirty years to the same man."

"Jesus Christ," someone at the bar shouted. "The fucking guy must be blind, deaf, and dumb!"

That set the crowd off on another round of jeers and flying peanuts.

"So, you are against the Family Vow?" Foxglove asked, hoping she would say something they could tear apart for the next half hour of the program.

Dickey forced a wider smile. It was known she had been told by her media advisors to smile at every question. It was necessary to break the commonly held belief that she was tough as nails. "I don't think it's my place to tell people how to live."

"No, bitch!" a man at Casey's Sports Bar shouted at the TV. "Your place is right here," he said and grabbed his crotch.

That, of course, brought raucous laughter, more boos, and an avalanche of peanuts thrown toward the monitors.

"I just love this crowd," I said to Abe. I took another sip of my martini, which I had to admit was pretty good. "Look at this crowd. They're so dumb, they'd even elect me President."

"You gott'a be kidding," Abe said. He said it too fast. I knew and he knew where this would go.

"Yes, me," I went on. "Why not me? Look at me. I'm telegenic. I can talk out of both sides of my mouth. I have unlimited funds. Christ, Abe. With the right spin," I winked, "and a little spice, they would clamor to elect me."

"They're not *that* dumb," Abe said softly, not so sure himself.

I smiled. "Wanna Bet?"

Reluctantly, Abe replied, "Okay."

"But no interference from you!"

6

At noon on July 15, 2016, I started my campaign for the presidency. No one knew it but I.

My long black limousine pulled up outside 2331 Broadway. That was the rent-controlled building I had intended to pull down so I could build a high-rise luxury apartment building.

There were about thirty pickets walking in their circle in front of the entrance to the building. The protesters were carrying signs as they walked in a small circle in front of the entrance of the building. Some said DAVID SAVAGE IS A BLOOD SUCKER. Other signs said SAVAGE IS THE DEVIL. All the protesters shouted either "Blood Sucker," or "Savage is the Devil."

I rather liked the signs that said I was the Devil, but I must admit I have never sucked anyone's blood. That would be in the line of work for some misguided human.

The minute I stepped out of the limo, the pickets started shouting, "Blood sucker, blood sucker."

It had been a slow news morning and KWDR, one of the local television stations, had sent a crew to film the protest. I was always good copy, and they were looking for a small story for the 6 o'clock local segment.

Mercedes Lopez, the reporter assigned to the piece, spotted me and told Dough Fitzgerald, her cameraman, to zero in on me.

I had just reached the sidewalk and was maneuvering around the protesters toward the entrance of the building. Suddenly I bolted through the protesters and into the street. The camera, I knew, was right on me. I stepped between two cars and took hold of a pregnant woman and shoved her into the arms of a protester as a bus came hurtling by.

The camera captured it all: me falling in front of the bus; shouts and gasps from the protesters; me on the ground after the bus had passed; me standing up, brushing myself off.

The protesters rushed over to me. Some brushed the debris off my clothing; all praised me for my heroic action.

"You're my hero," an elderly woman protester pinched my cheeks.

"It was nothing," I said demurely and continued to clean the dirt off my suit.,

Lopez and her crew edged closer. This was no longer filler. This would be the lead story.

A young, bearded, male protester, who had come to walk the picket line with his grandfather, walked up to me and extended his hand. "That was awesome, man."

"I only did what anyone else would have done," I said, shaking the man's hand long enough for the TV crew to get it.

Lopez shoved the microphone in front of my face. "I don't think so," she said, breathlessly. "That was really brave."

"Just being a good citizen," I said, winking at Abe, who had come across the street from the deli.

"So when did you become so nice?" Abe asked.

"Nice! I've always been nice. You don't see that. You've always resented me because I have all the fun."

"What fun?" Abe asked.

"You came out first and decided you would be God, and I had no choice but to be the Devil. Now you resent me."

"Why would I resent you?"

"Because you don't have a sense of humor."

"What? Telling everyone that Eve came from Adam's rib. You don't think that was funny?" Abe started walking me across the street to the deli. It was Tuesday, and I always had lunch at the deli on Tuesday.

7

Kandinsky's Upper West Side Delicatessen, Kosher since 5720, is on the ground floor of 2350 Broadway, a 1903 five-story brick tenement. If you were to investigate the ownership, you'd find that the papers in the New York City Building Department attest that Abe Kandinsky bought the building and the restaurant on the ground floor in 1959. Above the restaurant are barbell apartments on each of the four floors. They are called barbell apartments as they are shaped like a barbell, 2 apartments in the front and 2 in the back. The ones in the back are a bit smaller than the ones in the front, and their toilets are in the hall.

Should you care to investigate further, the records indicate that Abe got the required licenses to reconfigure the restaurant into a kosher deli.

I would call the deli New York 50s style: white Formica tables with skinny metal legs. Chairs with the same metal legs with cracking red vinyl cushions. A counter with the same Formica top and bar stools with spindly wooden legs and red vinyl cushion tops.

You could walk past the deli blindfolded and know it was a kosher delicatessen. It was the combination of the spicy hot dogs and sauerkraut boiling, and the pastrami steaming. The working area behind the counter had huge slabs of pastrami and corned beef, which the men working there would carve into four-inch high sandwiches.

The only thing that had changed from the fifties was the men working the steam tables. In the old days, they all were Jewish. Now they were Puerto Rican, Black, and Chinese—all of whom spoke enough Yiddish to make the older customers feel right at home.

Abe sat me at my usual table by the window. "Nice work." He couldn't help grinning from ear to ear. "Some stunt!"

"Yes," I agreed. "It had a rather earthly quality to it. Not too dramatic."

"Oh, no. For you... not too dramatic. Look what you started." Abe gestured to the media crowd that had gathered outside the deli's door.

"What are you complaining about? It'll be great for business."

"I don't need more business."

The good thing about our betting was that there was never any malice. It was a game and we were pretty much equal as long as he didn't butt in. He did have a few tricks more than I did.

"So the same." Abe smacked the edge of the table with the white (that's a misnomer) kitchen towel he always held under one armpit. I remember when we first saw that gesture. It was over a hundred years ago. We were eating at Ratner's on the Lower East Side when it really was the Lower East Side of poor Jews and immigrants.

"The same?" Abe asked and smacked the table again.

"Guess?"

"I'm too tired to guess," Abe answered, putting on his weary voice and seeming to grow a little smaller.

I made clicking sounds with my tongue. "Abe, you're not as much fun as you used to be in the old days. You're getting old."

"My arthritis is killing me."

"You know you don't need to suffer."

"I'm looking older, and you look younger every day." Abe went back into his whining mode. Growing impatient, he smacked the table again as if it were a disobedient child that would not respond.

20

"Okay. Today I feel Jewish so I'll have herring, an everything bagel, slightly toasted, coleslaw, a few pieces of potato salad, and a beer. And when I'm done, a knish for dessert."

Abe left and Evie came up to the table next to me. Evie is a middle-aged African-American woman who has worked there for years and I knew had a crush on Abe. She was delivering a hot pastrami sandwich and cream soda to Meyer Horowitz, who seemed to be there whenever I was there. "Here, Honey," she said sweetly to Horowitz as she put the food in front of him.

"Nu?" he said. Horowitz was a retired school principal who was forever propositioning Evie.

Evie leaned down and gave Horowitz a sweet, innocent kiss on the cheek. She knew that's all he wanted. His talk was all bravura now, playing an old tape from long ago.

I, too, had tried but was no more successful, even less. I never got a kiss. I would hit on her every once in a while. She didn't like me and made no bones about it. She came and stood at the end of my table and glared at me. "Wha you want with Abe?"

"Nothing," was my pleasant answer.

"You leave that man alone," she demanded. "I know you—you up to no good."

By then Abe came by with my order and brought a plate piled high with chopped chicken liver and several pieces of rye bread. As he went to sit with me, Evie put her hand out. "Don't sit. He ain't no man. Smells like sulfur."

Abe sat and we both laughed. "So I smell like sulfur," I said. "Wonder where she got that idea?"

Abe spread a glob of chicken liver on a slice of bread and then put some mustard on it. Before he put that in his mouth, he said, "Ye gotta remember Evie's a church-going lady. She can smell the Devil in you."

"Moi," I cried indignantly, as I put some herring on my bagel. A few slices of onions and I was ready to eat. "Bet still on?" I asked and took a bite of my food. "Damn it, Abe, this is really good."

"Good?" Abe stammered. "What do you know from good?"

"Bet still on?" I asked.

"Of course." Abe took a sip from my beer. "You know I never go back on my word."

I couldn't help myself but laugh at that. Almost choked up a piece of herring. "Yeah, your word. We all know about your word and the trouble it has caused."

That pissed him off. He picked up his bread and chicken liver and hobbled back to the kitchen.

I looked out the window at the media crowd. I waved and they screamed questions at me. Had them where I wanted them. I was on my way.

8

That evening Abe and Evie were sitting in the deli's back room office. It was a small room, jam-packed with boxes with receipts from the time the deli opened. The wallpaper was peeling and several framed posters—one of Mickey Mantle, another of Roger Maris—were barely clinging to the wall. Abe sat in an ancient wooden swivel chair in front of his desk, one leg draped over the edge. Every time he moved the chair squeaked.

Evie was sitting on a well-worn small sofa drinking beer out of a bottle. Abe had refused a beer—wasn't in the mood to drink.

I, so to speak, was the proverbial fly on the wall.

They were all watching the 6 o'clock evening local news on KWDR-TV. On the screen was Matthew Levinson, the anchor, excitedly exclaiming, "We are watching one of the great turnarounds in this city's history. David Savage, the well-known and generally maligned developer has stopped at nothing to get what he wants. We have Mercedes Lopez on the scene."

The scene showed Lopez in front of the tenement building.

"What caused Savage to do a complete turnaround?" Levinson asked off camera.

"No one is sure." Lopez looked earnestly at the camera. This was her moment. She already saw herself as the next female anchor at KWDR. "All we know is that Savage sent word to the tenants committee that he will do nothing to the building until all the rent control tenants leave." She took in a deep breath. "And that could take years!"

On the screen, the camera panned to the pickets on the street, most of whom were all smiles as they went through the process of tearing up their protest signs.

Lopez walked over to one bearded young man who was angrily waving his sign at the camera. "What do you think of Mr. Savage's decision?" Lopez asked him.

"He's a shit," the young man shouted. "I don't trust him. He's a capitalist pig. He rides on the backs of the poor."

"But hasn't he decided to let the poor people stay in the building?" Lopes asked incredulously.

"He's not helping anyone—only himself."

"But you'll be able to stay there. You are young. You can stay under rent control for a long time."

"I wouldn't be caught dead in one of his buildings."

"You don't live here?" Lopez asked.

"No way."

"Then why are you here?"

"I'm a Trotskyite, here to help the oppressed."

The screen showed Lopez walking away and caught her muttering to herself, *"I'm not sure what a Trotskyite is. Perhaps a professional picketer?"*

Lopez walked over to an elderly woman holding her husband's hand and crying. Lopez shoved the microphone into her face. "What's your reaction to the news?"

"My reaction, sweetie?" the woman asked. Wiping her tears she said, "I love David Savage. He's an angel. As far as I am concerned, he knows about what people want. He's the one who should be running for President."

Lopez faced the camera and spoke my words coming out of her mouth. "So there you have it," Lopez's voice was full of gravitas; she had already elevated herself to an analyst. "In one swift move, David Savage goes from being the Devil to a Presidential candidate."

9

Corporate headquarters for Savage Enterprises occupies the top five floors—82 through 86 of Savage Towers Downtown. I, of course, have an enormous corner office that takes up half the floor. One side of windows frames downtown Manhattan and the financial towers of Wall Street. Another side of windows looks out over high-rise office and apartment buildings stretching to the East River.

Naturally, the office is expensively furnished: a highly polished wooden floor with a smattering of oriental carpets, soft leather chairs, an informal conference area, and a far wall of brass-trimmed bookcases.

I decorated the room myself. After all, who has better taste? Mostly artifacts from great empires of the past: an ancient dented helmet from Sparta; a marble bust of Caesar, supposedly done in his lifetime; a prayer rug from Isfahan; several volumes of war annotated by Napoleon.

My most important possession is a life-sized gray marble statue of a man that stands across from my desk in a corner between a glass-enclosed pharaonic death mask and a painting of George Washington at Valley Forge.

The statue is similar to many sculpted in the Archaic style, 615–550 B.C., in Greece. The man's face has eroded over time, his nose partially missing, perhaps like the Sphinx, shot off by an alien invading army. The statue is nude, frontal, its penis hacked off most likely by a conquering Muslim, symbolically emasculating the local male population.

Aside from that, the figure is in good shape: a square-shouldered youth with a narrow waist, strong legs, and feet planted flat on the ground, the left foot in front of the other, striding. His arms are muscular, powerful, and stiff at the sides of his body, hands clenched in fists.

Most authorities would call the statue a Kouros, a youth, and let it go at that. Not I. I found the statue in Cyprus and knew it immediately. It was a statue of a slave. Not just any slave. I had been that slave.

I had five flat screen TVs scattered throughout the room, each turned to a different channel, each a jumble of quickly changing images. There were no sounds from the TVs. All the noise, high-decibel hip-hop music, came blasting in through speakers at the corners of the room.

Without knocking, Bruno Fuscati came into the room through a side door, paneled to look like part of the room and not a door. He waved to me. "Hayadooin?" he said, but didn't wait for or want an answer.

I watched him cross the room to a full-length wall cabinet that housed a refrigerator. He opened the door, which revealed a full-sized refrigerator filled with champagne bottles, nothing else. He pointed to a Krug '69 and looked at me.

"No. Let's do the '07 Heidsieck."

That brought a big smile to Fuscati's face. He picked up some flutes and walked over to my desk. Fuscati is what in his area of Brooklyn would be called a *Cugine*, a slick, Saturday Night type of guy: beautiful young man, almost too Botticelli/Bacchus beautiful, dressed in tight jeans, a yellow shirt open at the neck with rolled up sleeves to emphasize his exceptional biceps… and to display his tattoos running down both arms to his hands. He's always wearing red crocodile cowboy boots. His muscular chest serves as a platform for several thick gold necklaces. His long hands have rings on every finger, and his wrist sports bracelets in gold, copper, and silver.

Fuscati advanced toward my desk, dancing to the music and carrying the champagne and glasses.

I took a glass and he poured. "So what's da fucking occasion?" he asked. His voice was gravelly as if he needed a pure Brooklyn accent to accentuate his scariness.

Fuscati usually brings a big smile to my face. For millenniums people have believed the Devil comes to Earth with his coterie of impish demons. Never needed to. I can always find enough "demons" on Earth to help me in my work.

"Your news first," I answered and took a sip of one of the greatest wines ever produced in the world.

"Dickey is so way ahead of da pack. Da Democrats won't change her for yo, no matter what yo lay on dem. Dey ain't gonna crumble."

"And the Republicans," I asked staying focused on the tastes in my mouth.

"What a foocking joke. Each week der's a new scutch at the top of the heap. I say, let them foocking eat each other and yo have fun with the crumbs."

"Which leaves us with the Libertine Party," I saluted Fuscati with my glass.

28

"Yea," Fuscati smirked. "Deys got the right name for us." He poured more champagne into my glass and refilled his. "Dey dumb, boss." Fuscati put the champagne bottle on my desk and took a sip from the glass he was holding. "Dey assholes and don't stand a chance."

"I like the odds," I answered and raised my glass. Fuscati came around the desk and we clinked glasses. "I like the odds," I repeated and took another sip of wine.

"Yea and guess wha?"

"I'm all ears."

"Dey on de ballots in every state."

"Sweet!"

"So, boss, wha we gonna do?"

10

I offered my glass up to Fuscati who filled it. I picked up a remote control, shut off the music and all the monitors except one and on that, I found "The View."

The screen showed the four women, two on each side of Bryon Benson. "So," Whoopi Goldberg asked Benson. "Why are you running when it appears you have no more chance than a snowball in—" Hell got bleeped out.

The camera focused on Benson. Before he could open his mouth I looked intently at him on the screen and whispered, "America needs an alternative to the business as usual politicians. We need someone totally different."

In the TV studio, Benson opened his mouth and said, "America needs an alternative to the business as usual politicians. We need someone totally different."

"But," Goldberg rolled her eyes, made a face, and pursued her line of questioning. "What can you offer America that the other candidates can't?"

I silently spoke to Benson through the TV monitor.

Out over the airwaves to millions and millions of Americans and to the cable news networks that had a field day with his answer, Benson said, "I would be the first openly gay American President."

11

The next morning I came out of my apartment building with a beautiful woman on each arm: a blonde on the right, a brunette on the left.

We were immediately surrounded by a horde of reporters and television crews. A young woman reporter shoved her microphone into my face. "Is it true, Mister Savage?"

A male reporter asked, "Any comment?"

I smiled. "Comment about what?"

The female reporter pushed her way back to the front of the pack. "That you are considering running for President on the Libertine Party ticket."

My smile grew wider, my eyes twinkled. I looked directly into the camera. "Who told you that?"

Another male reporter elbowed his way to the front. "It's all over the political blogs and social media."

I didn't respond. I moved through the crowd with the two women toward my limo waiting at the curb.

The woman reporter was at my heels. "Who are the women?"

I turned around to the two women. "Oh, how impolite of me." I nudged the blonde toward the media pack. "This is Honey. She was the 2015 Playmate of the Year."

I pulled Honey back and gently coaxed the brunette in front. "This is Melody. She was January of this year."

All the reporters starting shouting questions at me, but I ignored them and escorted the two women into the waiting limo.

I could hear the reporters wildly speculating about the women and me. The limo started and I could see the reporters and cameras following it. "George," I said to my driver, "go about twenty feet and then stop."

When the limo stopped, I got out of the car and started walking up the street. The reporters and television crews were running after me. I walked to a young male dog walker holding onto the leashes of ten medium- and large- sized dogs. Approaching the pack of dogs was an elderly woman with her Jack Russell on a leash.

The Jack Russell lunged at one of the dogs, which set the whole pack on the little dog. They encircled the Jack Russell. All the leashes got tangled. The elderly woman dropped her leash. The Jack Russell was caught in the middle of the pack, which the dog walker couldn't restrain. The pack was barking furiously. The Jack Russell stopped, barked, assumed the position, and took a dump.

Once the Jack Russell was done, I maneuvered through the leashes, leaned in, and picked up the Jack Russell. I handed the dog to the elderly woman. I then removed my silk breast pocket handkerchief and picked up the dog's poop.

The cameras never stopped rolling. The reporters, however, were speechless. I tied the ends of the handkerchief into knots and slowly walked over to a rubbish can. I nonchalantly threw the handkerchief in. I paid no attention to the cameras or the reporters who had regained their ability to shout. I blithely walked back to the limo, got in, and we drove off.

Even before the limo had gone two blocks, there were videos racing across the news cable shows as "BREAKING NEWS."

12

Lillian Stillworth hosted the early afternoon *Noon Breaks* on MSBCS TV. Lil, as she preferred to be called, was a tall patrician woman of a certain age with impeccable American credentials. From the Mayflower to Independence Hall to all the wars America has fought, the Stillworths had leading roles. Lil's father had been the Ambassador to France and Lil grew up not only bilingual, but bicultural, and rumor had it she was also bisexual. France had given her a long-term view of the world, a view that was tempered by hundreds of years of literature, fashion, and most important, the use of wit.

Usually, Lil interviewed celebrities from the world of the movies, fashion, or the arts. Today, however, she was alone in her studio that resembled a chic apartment that could be anywhere in the moneyed world. She was in her signature pose: sitting in a Louis XIV "loveseat," wearing an ancient, yet elegant, Chanel suit. The index finger of her right hand was hooked around three strands of very large pearls. She looked straight at the camera.

"So?" She exaggerated her very upper crust accent. "What was it? Hermes? Valentino," she paused and pursed her lips, and spoke somewhat disparagingly, " or just a Polo?"

In the CASBC TV studio set of *After Noon*, Lawrence Richter looked into the camera and asked, "The question on everyone's mind… what qualifies David Savage to run for President?"

Richter paused, took off his eyeglasses, and twirled them in one hand. He turned around and looked at the huge monitor behind him. "To answer that, we have Sherman Oxenhammer, Abel Carran's chief strategist."

Oxenhammer appeared larger than life on the screen. He was a big man and the wide-angle monitor made him even wider. He was in his mid-sixties, florid-faced, large nose, large ears, and what was obviously a very bad hairpiece. Oxenhammer suffered from some unnamed follicle disease that had made his hair grow every which way. He usually gelled his hair down and then put on his hairpiece. Unfortunately for him, the gel had not held; neither his hair nor the piece stayed down. He knew his hair was wrong, but he never missed a chance to show his face on television.

"I can't see this David Savage as a viable candidate," Oxenhammer said in his deep gravelly voice.

"But people seem to love him." Richter had no trouble creating truth out of whole cloth. In fact, that was his stock in trade.

"Look, that's all he is: a fresh face," Oxenhammer countered. "You can't run a government with a pretty face."

Over at the TCN TV studio, Raymond Foxglove, the anchor of many of their shows was saying, "Be sure to join us for *The Missing Point* this evening for an in-depth look at David Savage. Now, we have Richard A. Hyman, Governor Dickey's campaign manager on the line."

The picture going out was split in two. On one side was Foxglove and on the other side was a photo of Hyman. He was a handsome man in his mid-forties with a wide smile on his face. He looked as if he hadn't a trouble in the world.

"What do you think of David Savage's chances of running for President?" Foxglove asked.

The photo of Hyman remained on half the screen as his voice came over the audio. "First of all, he doesn't have the nomination."

"But that could easily change," Foxglove offered. "The Libertine Party has had no candidate since Benson."

"Look, Ray," Hyman's voice became familiar, friendly. "This is a joke. It's the media making him something he is not. He's not a politician. Perhaps a celebrity. That's all he is and you can't run a government with a celebrity."

At the MSCBS set of *Noon Breaks*, Stillworth was signing off, replaying the video of me picking up the dog poop. "Here's the latest," she said, before the screen changed. "We've been told that in the last two hours the video has gone viral with over twenty million hits on YouTube."

1 3

At 11p.m. EST the cognoscenti watched *The Nightly Show*, hosted by Stu Golden. It was his irreverent, but factual, look at the news that made him so popular. He never created news. He simply took what people in the news, mostly politicians—were saying and put their words and actions in contexts that revealed how unethical, unreal, and unconnected they really were.

After the opening monologue and a commercial break, the camera focused on Golden sitting at his desk sipping from a coffee mug. I knew that the mug was filled with añejo tequila. Golden was wearing a blue suit, blue shirt and a light purple tie with diagonal, London School of Economics stripes in purple, black, and gold. All a perfect offset to his graying hair.

"Now," he started, putting a serious look on his face, "for our newest segment." The screen filled with a cartoonish drawing of the White House and the words: *CLUSTER#$#$$ to the WHITE HOUSE.*

The camera went back on Golden laughing at his own joke. "Is there a viable third party candidate?" he asked, quickly putting on a serious demeanor. "There is breaking news and let's see what the news pundits have to say."

Golden looked to his right and the screen was filled with four different cable news anchors. The camera zoomed in on a full-length shot of TCN's Foxglove. "What does David Savage know about running a government?"

Then the camera went to Myron Path, who hosted *Newsmakers* on MSBCS. Only Path's head was visible. His eyes were close-set and he sounded as if he had a cold. "What does it mean to have a third party?"

The camera moved on to Richter at CASBC in the third box. "Is the country really ready for a third party?"

The last box had the very large Eastern European face of Igor Olshansky, public television's political analyst on BBTT. "The country is ready for something different." Olshansky's voice was like timber falling in the woods. "Democrats and Republicans are facing a political tsunami."

The camera went back to Foxglove for the last quote. "There's no question the old political party's brands are in trouble. In a funk; you could say they are in the toilet."

Golden had the full screen to himself. A wry smile crept over his face. You could feel the tension in his body, trying to keep from laughing. "And who's the man to clean up all that shit?"

The screen showed the video of me picking up the dog's poop.

14

A blacked-out, black stretch limo slowly made its way through Central Park. In the back seat, Sherman Oxenhammer and Richard A. Hyman sat sipping fifty-year-old scotch that Oxenhammer kept in his car. The window to the chauffeur's seat was closed, and Oxenhammer knew Melvin couldn't hear what was being said.

"Do you know why I like to meet you this way, Sherman?" Hyman asked in a friendly tone.

"The scotch," Oxenhammer answered and took a long sip from his cut crystal glass.

"Well," Hyman said, knowing how much store Oxenhammer put into his scotch offerings, "yes, that and the fact that we do see eye to eye about the political process."

"We need to stop him... stop him, Dick."

Hyman winced. He never liked to be called *Dick*. It was too much with a name like *Hyman*. But he said nothing.

Oxenhammer went on: "Stop him before it gets out of hand."

Hyman sipped his scotch. He agreed about stopping me, but wanted the suggestion to come out of Oxenhammer's mouth, just in case this was being recorded. He was sure it wasn't, but... "How?"

"I'm thinking," Oxenhammer answered, but his mind drew a blank. I suggested something to him. Oxenhammer suddenly thought *he* had the idea. He didn't know where it came from, but it was perfect. "Let's do what our friends in the media always do."

"Meaning?" Hyman asked. He had no idea what Oxenhammer was thinking.

"We'll demonize him."

15

It was a beautiful evening in New York. There was a gentle wind coming across Central Park toward the encampment of television crews on either side of the entrance to my apartment building on Fifth Avenue. The police had set up barricades to keep the media as far back from the entrance as possible. Of course, all to the annoyance of my neighbors in the building who complained to me loudly.

Across the street, on the Central Park side of Fifth Avenue, Jonathan Latour, a clean-shaven, carefully groomed young man, slowly paced back and forth. He was wearing a black suit, white shirt, and narrow black tie. His wing tip black shoes were polished to a high gloss. There was nothing about Latour that was unusual, other than the fact that he looked like a Mormon proselytizer, which might not draw anyone's attentions, except for the sign he was carrying.

It was a plain white cardboard sign. At the top in bold letters, he had written THE END IS NEAR. Below that, in larger letters was THE DEVIL IS SAVAGE.

Bored with waiting for some sign of me—I was upstairs in my apartment but knew exactly what was going on in the street—Molly Worth, a TCN reporter, thought she should cross the street with her cameraman. So she did—and approached Latour.

Walking alongside Latour, Worth asked, "Why are you carrying that sign?"

Latour continued his pacing and without looking at Worth said, "Because it is the truth."

"Did someone send you here?" Worth asked, this time thrusting her microphone at Latour.

His reply was simple: "I am doing God's work."

Worth had a gut feeling there was a story here. So did the other reporters when they saw her talking to Latour. The reporters and their camera crews made a mad dash to cross Fifth Avenue.

At the same time, the light had changed up ahead, and a phalanx of cars came barreling down Fifth Avenue. They couldn't stop in time and went crashing into the reporters and camera crews on the street.

Worth and her cameraman turned when they heard the screeching noise of brakes and rubber, followed by yells of pain and anguish. She started screaming hysterically. Her cameraman just kept shooting.

"Oh my God, Oh my God," Worth kept screaming, holding her hands to the sides of her face.

She felt a hand on her shoulder and stopped screaming. She turned and saw it was Latour.

There was the slightest satisfied smile on his face. "I told you so."

16

In the BBTT television studio, the red light went on and Olshansky looked into the camera. "Good evening. I am Igor Olshansky, bringing you this breaking news." At the bottom of the picture, the words *Breaking News* kept scrolling by.

"We have just learned that the police are questioning a Jonathan Latour, the young man who was holding up the sign before the accident."

Footage of the accident played on the large monitor behind Olshansky, focusing down to Latour with the sign.

"We have been told by a confidential police source that Latour has admitted to being a member of a Devil- worshipping sect called the Phistos."

17

The cleaning crew was mopping the tile floor of the deli. Abe had gone into the office and was sitting in his old swivel chair at the desk. Evie came in with two beers. She leaned forward on the desk and took a swig from her bottle.

"Here," she said, handing him the beer.

"Don't feel like it," Abe replied without looking at her.

"I don't know why." Evie leaned over and ruffled through his mop of white hair that hadn't been combed in days. "You a little glum tonight?"

Abe didn't respond.

"Why don't I come up tonight?" Evie asked in a sweet voice.

Abe looked at her. He liked her, always had. But... "Why do you keep asking?"

"Because I want to go to bed with you."

Abe picked up his beer. He didn't want any. He just didn't want to have this conversation. He took a sip and put the beer back on the table. "Come on, Evie. I'm an old man," he finally said.

Evie laughed. "Honey, you may be old, but I sense a lot of energy tucked away inside you—just inching to get out." She tipped her beer to Abe. "Tell me, Honey, have you been with a woman since your wife died?"

"Yeah, since my wife died," Abe mumbled. He never had a wife, of course. All that was put together when he took on being Abe Kandinsky. No need to explain it to Evie. He picked up his beer and took a long swig. *No*, he thought, *not since his wife died.* Never! He had never been with a woman.

Abe picked up the remote and turned on the television. It was on TCN. *The Missing Point* had just started. Foxglove was sitting in a chair next to a table. There was another man in the chair opposite him, a man in a black suit and turned collar, a man with a face as if set in stone.

"Good Evening," Foxglove started with a serious voice. "Tonight my guest is Monsignor Francis Novak, a distinguished religious historian." Foxglove turned from the camera to face Novak. "What can you tell us about the Phistos?"

The Catholic priest faced the camera, his jaw set, his eyes black as night. His thin lips parted, and a deep sound came pouring out of his mouth. "There is no question but that they are a Devil-worshiping cult. They claim to trace their origins back to Lucious Phisto, who ruled the district of Languedoc in Southern France after Charlemagne deeded the land to him in 771 as a reward for fighting the Saracens in Spain."

"Charlemagne?" Foxglove exclaimed. "That far back?"

"Yes." Novak screwed up his eyes and his black bushy eyebrows elevated. He didn't like being interrupted. "A branch of the family became prominent members of a heretical sect of Devil worshippers in the tenth century. Many descendants were burned at the stake in 1323." Novak allowed himself a slight smile at that thought. "That had been done on the orders of Pope John XXII."

"1323?" Foxglove asked. "That far back?"

"Yes!" Novak spit out with an angry edge to his voice. "That far back!"

"How do you know all this?" Foxglove asked, although he knew the answer as Novak had told him all this before they went on the air.

"We know! The church has always kept close watch on them. We know some of them escaped and fled to Paris in 1330."

"And you think..." Foxglove paused. He wanted to be sure his audience was anticipating the question. "David Savage is a direct descendant of that same family?"

"We kept close tabs on them. Right after the French Revolution, they changed their family name." Novak stopped, waiting for Foxglove's cue that they had rehearsed.

"From?"

"From Phisto to Sauvage."

18

It was midday and I was sitting in my office. Fuscati came over with some flutes and a bottle of champagne. "Party down, Boss?" He poured some champagne for me and himself.

I raised my glass toward him. We clinked glasses. "Here's to being a political operative."

"Yea," Fuscati took a sip. "I drink to dat." There was a huge smirk on his face.

I emptied my glass of champagne and reached over to my intercom system and pushed a button. "Tell Buckley and Rosen to come in."

Whit Buckley and Ben Rosen were brought into the office. They were the co-chairs of the Libertine Party. They were about as different as cucumbers and watermelons. Buckley was a tall, thin patrician. He had been born right, had gone to the right schools, married the right woman, gone to work for the right law firm, and devoted himself to libertarian causes. Rosen was the son of Russian Jewish immigrants. He had gone to night school and worked full time for the New York City Housing Authority. He had gone to graduate school at night, became a teacher, specializing in American history. He'd written a score of books, lectured around the country, and had recently been named a university professor.

Fuscati greeted them and escorted them to the two chairs in front of the desk. I got up and shook hands with them. I introduced Fuscati and they shook hands. I suggested we go sit at the conference table, and when they sat down I offered them champagne, which they refused.

"You got the package I sent over?" I asked, pointing my index fingers at each of them like a pair of six-guns.

Buckley and Rosen nodded. "Yes, we got it," they said in unison.

"Then there's one new condition for me to become your candidate." I looked at Buckley and then at Rosen. "Are you sure you won't have any champagne?"

"No," Rosen snapped. He hadn't liked the idea of my pushing myself on them, sending over my ultimatum for being their candidate. Rosen had argued with Buckley long into the night, but Buckley was adamant. They had nowhere else to go, and I offered myself up on a golden platter. To Rosen, it was too generous an offer. He didn't trust me. "What's the new condition?" Rosen asked.

"My man here, Bruno, will be my campaign manager."

"But, David," Buckley said, his voice soft and conciliatory, "we already have a campaign manager. It's—"

I shot Buckley a glance that froze him in mid-sentence. "Yes, we do," I smiled. "His name is Bruno Fuscati."

Fuscati, who had been standing behind me, refilled my glass with champagne. Then he looked at Buckley and Rosen. "Yo boys got a problem with dat?" He made sure to flex his incredible muscles when he spoke.

19

The Missing Point opened with Foxglove holding a clipboard. He was standing in front of a narrow, raised table behind which his usual four panelists sat in front of their opened laptop computers, faces forward, eager to talk.

"So who is David Savage?" Foxglove threw the question at the panel.

"Who the hell is David Savage?" Harris Hillerman was the first to speak. He was a very large man, neck so wide it was busting out of his shirt collar. Aside from appearing on *The Missing Point*, he had a right-wing talk radio program that was syndicated across the country. Hillerman never minced words. "He's another sissy left-wing billionaire liberal New Yorker."

Megan Thrice brushed back her long blonde hair, and oozing sweetness at Hillerman said, "Maybe, but I think he's hot." Thrice had become one of the first celebrities of the right-wing conservative cause. She had decided in college that the only way she would make a name for herself was by being outrageous. So she twisted everything to suit her own advancement. The radio and TV talk shows loved to have her on. She could always be counted on to say something that was bound to go viral on the internet.

The camera was back on Foxglove. "We're trying to back this story."

"What story?" Hillerman barked.

"That David Savage is going to run for President," Thrice smiled and poked Hillerman in the ribs.

"If it's true." Thurston Clapp broke into the conversation. He was a former plumber and represented the *everyman* on the show. Four years before, at a televised town meeting, he had been chosen to ask a question to one of the Presidential candidates and the *every manness* (I would say stupidity) of the question made Clapp the sought-after man-in-the-street guy.

Everyone on the panel looked at Clapp. "If it's true," he repeated, "it could be a game changer."

The camera was back on Foxglove. "We're just getting dribs and drabs."

"Essentially, we're in a wait-and-see mode." Barnett Blessing, a columnist—more like a gossip writer—offered his assessment.

"Primarily the wait-and-see-mode starts right now." Foxglove summed up the discussion.

"How long does that last?" Clapp asked, looking at the other members of the panel for an answer.

20

I was sitting in the back of my limo watching *The Missing Point*. I switched it off, just as Clapp was asking, "How long does that last?" I answered him, "Till I say so, dummy." I reached for the bottle of champagne in the console on the side of the door and poured myself a glass. "Okay," I said out loud. "Are you going to show yourself?"

Abe answered, "I don't want your driver to see me."

"You haven't changed since the beginning of time," I laughed. "You know we can cloud men's minds. My driver can't see you or hear you or me unless we let him."

"I don't do tricks."

"Come on." My voice held all the aspects of exasperation. But I wasn't. Just acting in my human form. "Abe, you know it's only a trick if you do something unnatural. For us everything is natural."

No sooner had I said that than Abe was sitting next to me in the back of the limo. Abe looked around. "Not bad."

"You want a drink?" I pointed to the bottle of Dom Perignon '38. "It's a great year, and this is the last bottle in existence. Remember we had it in Paris after the liberation in '45?"

"What I remember," Abe's face lit up, "was the chanterelles at Tour d'Argent."

"So have a drink for old times' sake."

"You know I only drink on holidays."

"Yes, and what crap that kosher wine is."

"I have to set an example."

"What kind of an example? No one knows it's you."

"I know it's me."

"Oh, yes, I remember. I am that I am."

"So what are you going to do, boychick?"

"Win the bet." I poured myself more champagne and held the bottle out to Abe.

"No!" Abe shouted at me. "Why don't you ever listen to me?"

I chuckled. "I thought I might tempt you."

"Yeah. You got anything to eat?"

"I thought you'd never ask." I opened the small refrigerator and pulled out a beautifully wrapped box. "Here," I said, and handed it to Abe.

Abe didn't take it. "Looks too fancy for me. What is it?"

I slowly unwrapped the box. Inside were several small pieces of toast, and on each piece was a dollop of Caspian Beluga caviar. I picked one up and nibbled at it. "Delicious."

"No! You know, this is who I am." Abe poked himself in the chest with his finger. "I have to live this life as I am. What else do you have?"

I went back into the refrigerator and pulled out a mid-sized jar of pickled herring and handed it to Abe.

A big smile crossed Abe's face. "Now you're talking."

I handed Abe a fork. He opened the jar and started pulling pieces out of the jar and eating them. In between bites, Abe asked, "Nu! So when are you going to announce?"

"I'm planning my campaign even now." I turned the TV back on. The screen filled with a poster asking IS SAVAGE THE ANTICHRIST?

Foxglove read from his clipboard. "An online website said a poll showed that seventy-three..."

The screen showed the poster with the number *73* written in huge letters across it.

Foxglove continued to read. "Seventy-three percent of people polled said yes or maybe."

The top half the screen now had the words IS SAVAGE THE ANTICHRIST? The lower half had CALL IN TO VOTE—866-666-6666.

21

Olshansky's mid-day talk show, *What's on the Table*, was, like every other program, discussing me. "Is David Savage going to run?" Olshansky asked his two regular panelists, Joaqui Ingles, and Brent Ashenberger.

Ashenberger spoke first. "According to the Associated Press, David Savage will announce before the end of the week." The studio camera tracked to the monitors on the back wall, which showed the numerous stakeouts at my apartment and office buildings.

"Savage's lifestyle seems to have engendered a lot of blowback from the Christian Right." Olshansky commented on what the monitor was now showing: pickets carrying signs: "Savage is immoral," "Savage is the Devil."

Although it was past two o'clock, I was still in bed. And not alone. I was with two gorgeous women, a blonde and a redhead. We were watching *What's on the Table*. I turned from one woman to the other. "Girls, am I immoral being in bed with two women?"

"I don't know what immoral is," the blonde answered, "but whatever it is, you've got it, baby!"

Later that day, the two women and I were still in bed when I put the TV back on. This time I went to Path's show on MSBCS. Path was showing videos of the aftermath of the flooding in Iowa. "These are some of the pictures of the devastation in Iowa." He put a finger to his ear and announced that they had Abel Carran.

The screen filled with Carran standing on a hill looking down at a totally wrecked assisted living center. The cameras focused down to the elderly, milling around the destroyed facility—some in wheelchairs, some holding onto attendants, all with a glazed look in their eyes.

The reporter held out a microphone to Carran as he commented, "These people have no place to live. How can you help these people?"

Carran put a concerned look on his face. "First of all these people are in our thoughts and prayers. The local people are doing a wonderful job: the mayor, the sheriff, the volunteers who have made sandbags throughout the night. A ton an hour—"

A staff member whispered in Carran's ear.

"A ton a minute," Carran quickly corrected himself and grinned, all teeth into the camera. "A ton a minute. This is what I believe in—not government, but volunteerism and participation."

"But none of that has stopped the flooding," the reporter said. "And what about these people?" The camera focused in on the elderly who were wandering around, totally lost.

Carran moved and stepped in front of the camera. "I'm sure the Lord will work something out for them."

Enough of that. I switched to BBTC. Their cameras were focused on the other side of the senior center, where one of his reporters had a camera and microphone in front of Governor Dickey. "Governor," the reporter asked, "what can be done for these people?"

Dickey had been in Chicago and dashed over to Iowa as soon as she heard Carran was on his way there. She had a stern look on her face. "I will propose legislation to help these people."

The reporter was a woman who had worked for a liberal Congressman for several years. She left Washington because she got fed up with the unbridgeable gap between proposal and implementation. "But how will that help these people now?" she asked, using her microphone as a pointer toward the people milling around in the background.

Dickey held her ground. "On day one, I will offer legislation to set up quicker emergency responses."

"But, excuse me, Governor, didn't you cut funds in your own state for flooding emergencies?"

Before Dickey could answer, I switched back to Olshansky, who was breathless with the announcement, "We have David Savage on the line."

The TV screen had been split in two: on the left side were real-time aerial videos of the devastation and the elderly trying desperately to get to higher ground; on the right was a photo of me.

"Mr. Savage," Olshansky asked, "Do you have any thoughts about this situation?"

I put the speakerphone on and propped myself up in bed. I wondered what they would have done if we were on a live feed with naked women on either side of me. I looked at the TV monitor and said, "Which situation are you talking about?" I asked. "The flooding, the property damage, the lives of the people, or the situation where politicians turn disasters into photo-ops?"

"Ugh, ugh..." Olshansky gurgled. When he got his voice back he defended the politicians. "They are there to help those people."

"Are they?" I asked, my voice laced with sarcasm. "What are they using to help those people... prayers? If they believe in prayers, they should have prayed to God not to bring the flood. You know, He does have a tendency to do that sort of thing."

"What would *you* do?" Olshansky demanded.

"Have your cameras look further to the west."

The program director told his cameraman in Iowa to do that, and there on the screen was a fleet of helicopters off in the distance, moving in.

"I sent those helicopters," I said, pointing to the helicopters on the screen and then looked at the two women, one at a time. Each bent over and kissed me: the blonde on my right cheek, the redhead on my left cheek. I went on: "They will be picking up all of the 185 senior citizens who have lost their facility, along with the staff, and flying them to Waterloo Regional Airport where there is a plane waiting to take them to Miami."

"Miami?" Olshansky asked, totally perplexed. He felt I was playing with him. "What could they possibly do in Miami?"

The picture on the screen showed the helicopters landing and the elderly people from the assisted facility slowly moving toward them. I continued, "There they will be taken to the Caribbean Queen, the newest addition to my cruise ship company."

"Cruise ship?" Now Olshansky was angry. He was certain I was playing him for a fool. "What do they need a cruise ship for?" Olshansky asked, not bothering to modulate his voice.

"The ship was about to go on its shake-down cruise. I've ordered an additional crew of doctors and nurses for the ship, which will house all these people until their facility is rebuilt." The camera zoomed in as one by one the stranded elderly people were carefully taken aboard.

2 2

The picture of the helicopters taking the elderly was played over and over again on all the news networks and cable channels. It was the lead story everywhere.

The opening shot of *The Nightly Show* was a screen split in two. The left side was cut in half. The top half showed the helicopters picking up the people in Iowa. The bottom half showed the iconic video of the last helicopter leaving the American Embassy in Vietnam.

Golden was on the right side of the screen. "Maybe if Savage had been President then..."

* * *

Miles and Alice Wilson were sitting in the living room of their small frame house in Maine. With them were their daughter Maggie Kelly and her husband Brad.

Miles turned the sound down and turned to Alice. "Yeah, maybe. You know Alice, this sounds crazy but he looks like Alex Jimenez."

"You'll never stop thinking about him." Alice sighed deeply knowing how Alex Jimenez had changed Miles' life.

"He died in my arms," Miles defended himself.

"That was forty-five years ago," Alice replied harshly. "I keep worrying about today."

Miles turned away from her, embarrassed about the present.

"You lost your job, we're behind on the mortgage, you're unemployment is running out, Maggie and Brad have to live here with the baby. It's time you forget about Vietnam and think about what you have to do today."

"What can I do?" was Miles' meek response. Everything—Vietnam and unsteady employment—had sucked his ego, his strength, the manliness out of him.

"I'll tell you what you can do." Alice had married Miles before he went to Vietnam. She had told him to go to Canada and avoid the draft. He couldn't do that. He had to be there for his country. Since he got back, his country had done nothing for him. "It seems to me that the only one out there who seems to be getting anything done is David Savage."

"Savage?" Miles exclaimed.

"Yeah, Savage," Alice's voice rose. "I think he's pretty good. I'm going to work for him."

"Work for him?" There was an edge of anger in Miles' voice.

"Yes, work! You remember what that is? Maybe you should get a job and work for your family?"

"Oh, come on, Alice." Miles didn't like her talking this way in front of the kids. "I keep trying, but there ain't nothing out there."

"Maybe with Savage in the White House things will change."

"I can't vote for him," Miles protested, sucking air in through his lips.

"Why not, Dad?" Maggie looked up from the baby she was rocking in her lap.

"I'm a Republican," he answered proudly. "I've always been a Republican. My father was a Republican; my grandfather was a Republican. Jeez, we've been Republicans since the Civil War."

"Yeah, a Republican," was Alice's retort. "A lot they have done for the lower ninety-nine percent."

"Not much," Miles quietly admitted. "You're right."

"Damn right, I'm right. And I'm voting for Savage."

23

The Missing Point went on the air. As usual, Foxglove was in the center of the screen, holding a clipboard. "So who is David Savage, and is he trying to buy the presidency? For that, we turn to three gentlemen in our studio."

The camera focused on Sherman Oxenhammer as Foxglove made the introduction. "Sherman Oxenhammer is the chief strategist for Abel Carran."

The camera then moved to Richard Hyman as Foxglove said, "Richard A. Hyman, Governor Dickey's campaign manager."

Then the camera moved to Bruno Fuscati. "And now we have someone new, Bruno Fuscati, David Savage's—What is your official title?" Foxglove asked.

Fuscati raised a fist to the camera. In every sense he was the new body politic: good-looking, buffed, carefree, not particularly interested in the world at large. Not particularly intelligent, but street savvy; primarily looking to get whatever he could for himself. And, of course, looking to pursue his own pleasures, without too much cost.

"I assume you have been active in political campaigns before?" Before the show, Foxglove had his staff research Fuscati.

"Nah," Fuscati answered without any embarrassment and waved the question away. It didn't matter to him that he hadn't done this before. He felt right at home in the studio in front of the cameras. This is what he was destined to do. "Hey man, yeh, this is my first time. I'm like a virgin," he laughed.

"You have no experience in political campaigning?" Foxglove asked, as if surprised, knowing Fuscati didn't, but wanting to get that point across.

"It's un-American what this David Savage is doing," Oxenhammer broke in.

Hyman followed suit. "He can't just walk in here from nowhere and buy the presidency."

Foxglove turned to Fuscati. "Your response to that."

"Fock you, man," Fuscati snickered. "He's not buying the presidency. He's simply showing *can do*."

"As opposed to business as usual?" Foxglove offered, hoping to pit Fuscati against Oxenhammer and Hyman.

"Yea, man. That's right. Business as usual goes nowhere. Schifso! Hey man, look at me. I'm a risk taker. Americans are risk takers. David is Boss." Fuscati looked directly at the camera and raised his voice. "America, take a fucking chance. We're gonna win."

24

In a small walk-up apartment on Eldridge Street in the Lower East Side of Manhattan, Alisha Bishop, a 26-year-old vagabond/groupie was breastfeeding her six-month-old baby, smoking a joint, and watching the TCN broadcast.

"Motherfucker!" she screamed at the television when she saw Bruno Fuscati. "You son-of-a-bitch. You won't give me a penny for the baby and here you are strutting with all these assholes on TV."

* * *

In the studio, Thrice had turned to Fuscati, brushed back her long blonde hair, and said, "You're right, Bruno," in a seductively lilting voice. "We are risk takers. I love him. And who's he challenging? A mealy-mouthed sissy and a woman trying to prove her balls are bigger than any man's."

Fuscati brought his right fist up in a salute at Thrice. "Hey man, David Savage is the Man." He looked into the camera, and his eyes were on fire. "Take a chance, America! David Savage is offering America a chance."

"A chance?" Oxenhammer shouted. "A chance at what? He has no program. He hasn't spelled out any policies."

"That may be," Foxglove waved his clipboard in the air. "That may be, but the overnight polls have him at an astonishing approval rating of 17 percent and he's only been in the race... if he's in the race... for two days."

Hyman felt he should say something. "We don't even know if he is in the race. He hasn't announced."

"Oh, don't worry." Thrice swung her blonde hair around. "He'll announce. He's terrific."

Oxenhammer's face went red. He always thought Trice was his ally. He had pushed a lot of money her way. What the fuck was she doing? "What's so terrific about him?"

"Are you kidding?" Trice's face was flush too, but for different reasons. "He's hot!"

"You got that one right, baby." Fuscati put two thumbs in the air.

* * *

Bishop couldn't watch anymore. She was so angry. Her adrenalin soared through her body as the baby started wailing. Bishop picked up the remote and started changing channels. For some reason, she stopped at the *Murray Fisher Show*. On the screen was a woman about Bishop's age holding a baby. She was sitting in a chair, and two men were sitting in chairs, one on either side of her.

Fisher, a thin, balding man in his sixties, wearing a pair of slacks and a tight-fitting long-sleeve tee-shirt was standing in front of the threesome talking into the microphone he held in one hand. "In a minute we will find out who the real father is."

A written message filled the screen: If you are not sure who the father of your baby is, call 800-555-0090 and if you are chosen we will do the paternity test and have you and the man or men in question come on the program.

"That son-of-a-bitch, Bruno." Bishop started yelling at the TV again. "Keeps denying he's the father. I should fix his ass."

And then, for Bishop at least, the strangest thing happened. She thought her brain was talking to her. Of course it wasn't her brain. It was *me*: "Why don't you do it?"

Bishop answered out loud: "They'd never pick me. I never win anything."

"You never know until you try," I answered.

"Yah, that's right!" She picked up the telephone and started dialing the number.

25

The ballroom of the Waldorf Astoria Hotel was packed. It was the nominating convention for the Libertine Party. It was a foregone conclusion that I would be nominated, although I had not formally announced. No other name would be put into play. The ballroom was decked in American flags, and delegates held signs with my name.

Buckley and Rosen were greeted with a thunderous ovation when they walked onto the podium. In unison, they shouted into the microphone, "Welcome to the nominating convention of the Libertine Party."

The audience broke into a roar. The band started playing "Happy Days Are Here Again." The thousands in the ballroom were shouting, jumping up and down, and waving their banners.

All the networks and news channels were broadcasting the event. In the TCN studio, Foxglove looked into the camera and said, "This is it, folks. Originally, as you may know, not one news or cable network had planned to broadcast this event. All that has changed in the past forty-eight hours. David Savage has taken over the news; the war, the economy, unemployment, global warming, oil dependency, even *Dancing with the Stars* have been relegated to the back burner."

The image switched to the street outside the Waldorf Astoria. Pickets had been gathering for hours. The police, using barricades, had divided the pickets on either side of the main entrance to the Waldorf Astoria. Both groups were fundamental Christian, but with different points of view.

On one side, the protestors were waving signs that said, SAVAGE IS THE DEVIL, KILL HIM. Other signs had SATAN GET THEE BEHIND ME! Every sign was written in bold black letters.

Facing them on the other side of the police barricade was a different sort of Christian Fundamentalists. They all carried signs that read, SAVAGE IS THE ANTICHRIST, LOVE HIM. CHRIST IS COMING RIGHT BEHIND HIM.

"As you can see," Foxglove spoke, his image superimposed over the picture coming from the street, "David Savage has whipped up the passions. There's no middle ground between these two factions."

The TV director switched back to the ballroom and Buckley and Rosen. "Ladies and gentlemen," Buckley started. "Tonight is historic." Rosen took the microphone out of Buckley's hand. "Tonight we will nominate the next President of the United States."

The crowd burst into sustained cheering, hundreds of balloons flying into the air. The band started playing John Phillip Sousa's "Stars and Stripes Forever."

Buckley grabbed the microphone from Rosen. "You can guess who that man is. Names have been bantered about. But now I—"

Rosen took the microphone back. "We are here to ask that man to come out so you can nominate him by proclamation to be the candidate to run for President on the Libertine Party ticket."

The crowd went hysterical, cheering, stamping their feet, banging on their chairs, whistling. A couple of men used the madness of the moment to hug women next to them, making sure to grab their asses in the process.

Buckley put his arms in the air asking for silence. It took a while, but eventually the room became still.

Buckley got the microphone out of Rosen's hands. "Ladies and gentlemen, all of you here in the room and all of you out there in America, may I present the next President of the United States, David Savage."

The crowd went wild. I, looking rich, smart, and intelligent, my back straight, my head held high, strode to the podium. I shook hands with Buckley and Rosen, and then I faced the audience. I smiled. I waved. I nodded my head as if I were acknowledging individual members of the audience. I pointed my index finger at people, winking as I shot my finger at them. I allowed the demonstration to go one for a few minutes before signaling them to be seated.

The effect was dramatic. Everyone sat down. There was not a sound in the room. "This campaign," I started, "will be run on policy and commitment to a good program."

A tremendous cheer rose from the audience.

"It will not be run on speculation, personal agendas, or personal attacks." My voice was clear, modulated. I would be an orator this night. "The country—no, not the country—*our* country," I corrected myself, "needs to deal with real issues."

People leapt out of their seats, cheering wildly, clasping their neighbors at hearing the good news. All the television cameras captured their excitement and passion and sent that image to Americans across the country.

I asked for silence with my hands and got it immediately. "This campaign is not a virtual reality show. This campaign that we—you and I together—will wage is for real, and we need to be serious about what we present so the voters can make an intelligent choice."

A chorus of "CHOICE, CHOICE" went up from all over the ballroom. The chant grew louder and louder, accompanied by thousands of people stamping their feet.

"So to get to the real issues," I paused, waited until I had everyone's attention and then went on, "it is important that my first task before you tonight is to eliminate any areas for gossip, speculation, and innuendo."

The chant, "SAVAGE, SAVAGE" rose to a crescendo and stayed there until I motioned them to be quiet.

"To begin with—" I had thought hard about what my first comments would be. Now as I was about to say them, I was tickled at what I had come up with. My face, however, was a serene mask, revealing nothing, giving nothing away.

"I want to clarify two major areas of gossip and speculation that have begun to take on a life of their own. First of all, I have heard the comments about me being a bachelor, never having been married, and that I date women as a cover for being gay."

BOOS rang out from all over the room.

"I can tell you unequivocally that I am not gay." I paused and emulating Jerry Seinfeld with my hands outstretched and smiling said, "Although there is nothing wrong with being gay."

The room burst into laughter.

"Some of my best friends are gay, and I will admit that I tried it once but it wasn't to my liking."

The only sounds were the gasps of the television anchors.

"The other persistent rumor, which on the face of it, contradicts the other rumor, is that I run around with a lot of different women and that the country would not want a wild bachelor in the White House. So let me clear that up. First of all, I do love women."

The entire crowd in the ballroom at the Waldorf Astoria was on their feet shouting and whistling, "We love you, David, we love you, David."

26

Abe and Evie were watching the nominating convention on the TV in the office of the delicatessen.

"I don't like that man," Evie said, pointing to Savage on the screen. "But I wish you loved women half as much as he."

"I do love women," Abe protested.

Evie came and sat on Abe's lap. "Show me."

Abe wasn't surprised. He felt something like this was coming on. "I got a feeling this is going to be a long night." He gently pushed Evie off his lap. "Maybe I need a drink."

27

The crowd in the ballroom had quieted down and I went on. "But when I was thinking about accepting this nomination, I realized that this is not just another job, not just another company to run. The presidency of the United States is a sacred duty."

That brought the house down. The sustained cheering lasted a good five minutes. When it subsided, I said, "I want to guide this country back to its God-given greatness."

A thunderous ovation greeted those words. This is what everyone wanted to hear. This was what America was about, its God-given greatness.

"And I thought back to ancient times—what some would call the Golden Age. Those who were chosen to serve dedicated their service to the sacred. Dedicated not only their lives, but also the most important aspect of their lives: their celibacy. And so tonight, here is the pledge I make to you." I looked directly ahead, knowing all the people in the audience and all the people watching me on TV were waiting with baited breath. In a rounded, clear voice I announced, "I, David Savage, dedicate my celibacy to the office of the President of the United States."

28

Abe couldn't help but admire my performance. "What a piece of work," Abe blurted out as he took one of the two martinis Evie had made.

Evie clicked glasses and for a moment thought about sitting on Abe's lap. She backed off and sat on the small sofa. Wasn't the right time... yet. But she was determined—tonight was the night.

* * *

In the TCN studio, Foxglove's hands were spread as wide apart as his eyes. "Did I hear right?"

The monitor in the studio showed me leave the stage and walk around the ballroom. The crowd was electrified, everyone pushing, shoving, hands reaching out to touch me.

In the BBTT booth at the Waldorf Astoria, Olshansky was dumbfounded. "This is incredible."

In the MSBCS booth, Path was equally astounded. "No one saw this coming."

Foxglove looked at his panel of experts and asked, "A celibate in the White House?"

Thrice threw her long blonde hair back and with an ironic smile offered, "That will be the first promise he breaks."

"It's a trick." That was Blessing's profound thought.

Foxglove had recovered his astonishment. "But what a novel idea and they seem to love it."

The monitor showed the crowd going wild in the ballroom.

All the talking heads rushed to evaluate what I had done.

Path: "We were blindsided."

Ripstein: Who would have thought of this?"

Olshansky: "This is a game changer."

Richter: "Do you believe that crap about the sacred?"

Stillworth: "It was a powerful speech. Look at the way it affected the crowd."

All the stations followed me as I sauntered through the ballroom of the Waldorf Astoria. There wasn't a dry eye in the house.

Foxglove asked, "Where do we go from here?"

* * *

Abe had gulped down his martini. He held the glass out to Evie. "I think I need another drink."

"Me too," she said, and went to make two more drinks.

29

I had circled the ballroom several times and then made my way back to the podium. I raised my hands and smiled benignly at the crowd. "Please ladies and gentlemen, please be seated."

I waited till everyone was seated and quiet. Then I went on. "I also know that there has been a lot of speculation about my choice for Vice-President. First of all, I need someone who understands the problems of this country and is in agreement with me how we can fix what's wrong and improve what's right."

That brought the audience to their feet, cheering wildly.

When most of the people in the ballroom were seated, I began again. "I need a Vice-President who not only understands, but has the skill and the heart to get things to work, to get legislation passed, to get people involved in this, the greatest country in the world. We need a Vice-President who can listen to the people's problems and can get people to solve those problems."

It was almost too much for the crowd in the ballroom. It was as if they had become intoxicated. They were shouting, screaming my name. They were dancing. They were hugging, kissing: men to women, women to men, men to men, women to women.

I allowed the demonstration to go on for five, maybe seven minutes and then called for quiet. When I got it, I continued, "What I—what you—need is a Vice-President you can trust if anything were to happen to me."

Shouts of "No, No" rang out throughout the ballroom.

"Things happen," I answered calmly.

There were more shouts of "No, No."

I waited until the shouting subsided. "I don't believe anything will happen, and I do believe that we will win this election; and I as President and my running mate, the Vice-President, will do everything in our power to restore America to her rightful place in the world, restore our economy, restore our faith in our government—"

There was more cheering and shouting.

"...restore and repair the valiant efforts of our military—"

Sustained cheering and shouting from the ballroom.

"And we will shine like the city of God that we have always been, up on a hill for all the world to admire and emulate."

* * *

Inside the delicatessen office, Abe had finished his second drink and was feeling a little woozy. "I'm not used to this stuff. I'm getting a little light headed."

Evie went over and sat on his lap. She took his glass out of his hand and kissed his cheek.

Abe didn't resist.

"That's good," Evie smiled and started stroking his face.

"That feels nice," Abe said, and put one hand around Evie's waist.

* * *

Inside the ballroom of the Waldorf Astoria, the cheering had turned into a stampede. I kept gesturing for quiet, although I didn't want the demonstration to stop right away. When I decided it was time to go on, I forcefully pushed my open palms out toward the audience and there was total silence.

"So to help me and you through this time, I have chosen the most perfect Vice-Presidential candidate."

I turned to face the side of the stage as I spoke. "Please welcome the next Vice-President of the United States, Rue Williams."

30

There was pandemonium in the hall. Everyone was on their feet screaming, applauding, yelling, moving their arms and bodies, not knowing how else to express their joy.

Rue Williams, a beautiful middle-aged black woman, slowly walked onto the stage, kissed me, and waved to the crowd.

All Foxglove could say was, "I don't know what to say."

"He's a genius," Thrice added, smiling from ear to ear.

"What a choice!" As much as Olshansky didn't like Savage, he had to give him credit. "Everyone in America knows Rue Williams."

"My, God!" exclaimed Path. "The most famous black woman in America."

Richter added, "The most famous and richest woman in America."

The talking heads went on and on: "How did he do it?" asked Path.

"She'll have to leave her TV show," exclaimed Foxglove.

Stillworth was thinking about Rue Williams running for the office of Vice-President. "Rue Williams," she intoned, "is undoubtedly the most influential woman in the world. What a choice for Vice-President."

Williams and I stood at the podium smiling, holding hands, and raising then intermittently to acknowledge the roar of the crowd.

* * *

It was enough for Abe. He shut off the TV. He tried to get up but sank back down. He realized he was drunk. The first time it had ever happened. He couldn't understand how it had happened.

Evie helped him up and kept a hand under his arm, a very broad smile on her face. "Com'on honey. I'm gonna take you upstairs."

31

The Nightly Show opened with a picture of Williams and me standing at the podium in the Waldorf Astoria ballroom accepting the nomination for President and Vice-President from the Libertine Party.

A quick switch to Golden at his desk with a big smile. "Hey, wasn't that something? So what are the experts saying?"

The screen divided into quarters. Three of the quarters had videos from cable news shows. Golden was in the fourth quarter.

At TCN Foxglove said, "He's certainly changed the game."

At MSBCS Path said, "This is certainly a game changer."

Over at BBTT, Olshansky said, "The game is no longer the same."

Golden chimed in, "That's it?" He smiled and spread his hands. "Nothing else?"

Foxglove was shown saying, "It's already sending shock waves through the political establishment."

Path had this to say: "The political establishment will have a hard time dealing with this."

Olshansky raised the stakes, "It's a tsunami shaking up the political establishment."

With a quizzical look on his face, Golden asked, "Do they all have the same writers?"

* * *

The next morning, print and television ran headlines: "NO ONE SAW THIS COMING!" "REPUBLICANS AND DEMOCRATS SCRAMBLING TO COUNTER SAVAGE." "OVERNIGHT POLLS GIVE SAVAGE A THUMBS UP." "BOTH PARTIES HAVE SCRAPPED THE USUAL V-P SUSPECTS." "PARTIES ARE VETTING BLACKS, HISPANICS, WOMEN, EVEN A FEW ASIANS."

32

Pastor Wilfred Wiggins' Christ the Savior Church was just outside San Diego. Wiggins, a rotund man in his mid-sixties had been preaching for twenty-five years and had built his church from a tiny storefront into one of the largest mega-churches in the country. This particular Sunday, there were ten thousand people in his church and another four to five thousand sitting in cars in the drive-in parking pews that surrounded the church. The service was broadcast on massive monitors surrounding the parking pews.

Many people had suggested Wiggins broadcast on one of the Christian channels, but he had refused. He wanted his parishioners to be in the sacred confines of his physical church.

The choir had just finished when Wiggins, in his long black clerical robes, approached the podium in the center of the stage. He took his time to look out over his audience. He recognized many faces but didn't acknowledge them with a nod or a wink or a pointed finger. He never did when he was about to preach. He didn't want human contact to influence his connection to the Lord.

Pastor Wiggins closed his eyes and stretched out his arms. "Let us pray for divine guidance."

The pastor stood still, hardly breathing. His congregation sat quietly, not making a sound.

"Show us the way, dear God," Pastor Wiggins asked in round, ringing tones. It was more like demanding than asking.

The pastor waited a minute, two, and then he had a thought. He wasn't sure if it was a thought of his own, or that he was truly hearing the word of God. "Are you listening?"

Pastor Wiggins felt the electricity going through his body. It was the word of the Lord. "Yes, Lord, we are listening." Of course, it wasn't the Lord, it was me.

What Wiggins heard was. "He is an immoral man."

Pastor Wiggins knew this was from God. It was a sound so clean, so correct, so pure it had touched his heart. He couldn't wait to spread the good news. He opened his eyes and looked out at his congregation. They saw the fire in his eyes and felt the electricity.

"He," Wiggins roared, "is an immoral man!"

The audience of thousands rose as one and shouted, "Hallelujah! Hallelujah!" The thousands who were sitting in their cars watching the monitors caught the fire. They ran out of their cars, shouting, "Hallelujah! Hallelujah!"

Pastor Wiggins heard more and repeated the good news to his congregation. "He is the Devil doing the Devil's work."

The audience had stayed on their feet, hands in the air, praising the news with cries of, "Hallelujah! Hallelujah!"

Wiggins heard more and informed his congregation. "He has come to destroy America."

His congregation was ecstatic, shouting, "Hallelujah! Hallelujah!"

A question rose in Wiggins head and he silently asked, "Who, dear Lord?"

My answer came in an instant. Pastor Wiggins looked out over his congregation. He knew this was the greatest day of his life. He and the Lord were one. He took a deep breath and announced, "David Savage is the Devil. He is the Antichrist."

His words threw his congregation into a shouting frenzy. "Hallelujah! Hallelujah!"

"We must stop David Savage. He is no man. He is the Antichrist. He is the Devil!" Wiggins roared. He felt as if he had come down from the mountain, carrying the word of the Lord.

The ten thousand people in the church and the four to five thousand people in the parking pews roared their agreement, "Hallelujah! Hallelujah!"

33

At the same time, three thousand miles to the east, Harry Warfield was preparing to preach his Sunday afternoon sermon at Christ The Redeemer Church in Albany, New York. His church was on its way to becoming a mega-church. Not there yet, only three thousand members, but his following had been building over the past year.

Reverend Warfield was in his forties, long black hair and a perfectly sculpted face. He was tall, buffed, and good- looking. He could easily be mistaken for an athlete or a movie star. He had charisma. He had graduated from Harvard Divinity School and knew he was headed to become one of the leading ministers in his denomination.

Wiggins had foregone wearing formal clerical robes. He looked much better in his hand-tailored suits. He had a premonition earlier at breakfast that this would be an important day. He stood in front of his congregation, his arms outstretched, his eyes open. "Let us pray for Divine guidance." The reverend closed his eyes with his hands outstretched.

No sooner had he done that, then I sent him the call. "The Antichrist has come!" he announced in ringing tones.

The audience of men, women, and children rose as one, proclaiming, "Hallelujah! Hallelujah!"

While Reverend Warfield waited till everyone was seated, his mind was listening for more. When he had it, he announced, "We should rejoice."

Once again the audience rose, shouting, "Hallelujah! Hallelujah!"

He stopped listening. He had all he needed to know. He could take it from there. He looked out at his congregation, proud that he had been chosen to deliver the good news. "The Good Book says that the Antichrist precedes the second coming of Christ."

His congregations had remained standing and now chanted, "Hallelujah! Hallelujah!"

Reverend Warfield knew this was the moment he had been schooled for. His karma was meeting his destiny, and he would lead his congregation and all Americans to the return of God. "We must do everything to help this man."

Warfield took his time looking around at his congregants. He spotted men and women he knew. He winked at the women and nodded at the men. At the children, he pointed his finger as acknowledgment. Every look, every nod, every pointed finger sent a chill through his congregation.

"And who is the Antichrist?" the Reverend Warfield asked his congregation. He knew he was asking more than those in his church. He was asking all America. "Who is this Antichrist who will bring about the prophecy?"

Every eye in the church was on Warfield. Every ear was straining to get the good news.

Again I sent him the answer to his question.

"David Savage is the Antichrist, and we must help him in every way possible."

His congregation agreed with him. They knew they would be here for the Second Coming. "Hallelujah! Hallelujah!"

34

The *Larry Prince Show* had been on TV for thirty years. Prince was now in his late 70s, tall, thin always in a shirt and tie with very wide braces holding up his pants. The braces, in fact, were his signature piece. He had wide narrow shoulders, and the straps fit into a grove that had either been his natural anatomy or had been created with the years of wearing them.

He looked through his large-framed glasses at the camera and announced, "Tonight we have an exclusive first direct interview with David Savage since he became the Presidential candidate for the Libertine Party."

The camera swung from Prince to me. I was sitting across the desk. "Nice to be here, Larry."

Although Prince lived in Washington, D.C., he traveled to New York City quite often and on occasions had meet me socially. Prince was considered a "soft interviewer" in that he rarely asked the tough questions. He never wanted to. Controversy was not his style. He believed everyone had a point of view and his job was to be seen with the newsmakers. So it was a departure from his usual style when he said, "I would like to start with something that is on everyone's mind—the religious issue."

"Shoot," I smiled. It was a big warm smile that played on my handsome face. In fact, some talking heads were commenting that I was the first good-looking candidate for President since Kennedy.

"I read today," Prince glanced at the paper in front of him on the desk, "that the Reverend John Mather, the pastor of the twenty-six thousand-people mega-church and a major advisor to Abel Carran called you the Antichrist."

I was not surprised at the question, as I had put the idea into Prince's head. "Based on what facts, Larry?"

The words came out of Prince's mouth without him even knowing what he was saying. "Do you believe in God?" Prince asked.

"Of course I do." I had an image of Abe schlepping sandwiches out to the customers in the deli. "I know there is a God."

"Let me play the video of what happened outside your apartment building several weeks ago." The screen showed the cars piling into the reporters racing across Fifth Avenue. "It's kind of spooky. All that happened while that nut was carrying a sign that you are the Devil."

I smiled. "No, the sign said the Devil is Savage."

"Do you believe in the Devil?"

"The Devil?" I paused, and then went on. "We all believe in the Devil. It's the only way we can excuse some of the stupid things we do."

"And what happened that evening? Some people believe it—"

I interrupted him. "That it was the work of the Devil? Why not the work of God? Can we tell the difference?"

Not expecting to be quizzed, Prince changed the subject. "So is there a connection between you and Claude Sauvage?"

"Ah, Claude Sauvage," I said, as I held both arms out and then clasped my hands together and put them on the desk between Prince and me. "I am the perfect amalgam of France and America. Do you know that I can trace my American ancestry back to one of the founding fathers?"

"A founding father?" Prince was startled.

"Ten generations ago Benjamin Franklin fathered a child with his house servant Addie."

"Addie? Addie who?"

"She didn't have a last name. She had been one of Jefferson's slaves, and Jefferson gave her to Franklin to take to Paris when Franklin was appointed Ambassador to France." I paused and then went on. "She spoke French."

Prince was incredulous, but very happy. This was a real scoop. "A penny-saved-a-penny-earned Franklin?"

"Same man. Franklin acknowledged the child and legitimized him by having his footman—"

"Who was?" Prince breathlessly interrupted.

"Claude Sauvage. And yes, he was a Frenchman. He married Addie. Franklin bought them a house in Paris where the family lived until 1848 when Jean-Luc Sauvage, my great-great-great grandfather, left for America during the California Gold Rush and Americanized his name to Savage."

Before Prince could say anything, he heard a voice in his ear. He put one hand up in the air, signaling stop. His other hand went up to his ear, a finger pressing his earpiece.

Prince looked at me wide-eyed. "This is amazing."

I sat calmly smiling and slightly nodding my head, knowing what Prince had just heard.

Prince brought his hands down and put them both flat on the desk as he looked at me. "We have just gotten word that there was a sighting of the Virgin Mary in Latrobe, Pennsylvania. A Marsha McDonald saw the Virgin Mary coming toward her. She was wearing a blue cape and smiling and holding hands with David Savage."

35

Foxglove was standing in the center of *The Missing Point* set. He spread his arms wide. "So, what are we to make of Savage's news?" He turned to face his panel, seated behind a high table, their laptops opened.

"This is ridiculous," Blessing volunteered.

Megan Thrice smiled and announced, "I think it's fun!"

"What fun," Blessing glared at Thrice. "This is serious. We are trying to elect the President of the United States."

"Well, Barnet," Foxglove offered. "The people seem to like Savage."

"The people!" Blessing stormed. His face had turned beet red. "What do the people know? He hasn't made one policy statement. All he does is walk around—"

"Holding hands with the Virgin Mary," Thrice interrupted.

Clapp raised his hand and in his soft, hesitant voice said, "We still know nothing about him except that he is rich."

"Yes," Thrice's eyes were sparkling. "Very rich, but not as rich as Rue Williams."

"And certainly not as well known," Foxglove interjected. He glanced around his panel. "And what about the Rue Williams factor?"

"She'll bring in the fantasy vote," Blessing said sarcastically. "Voters will believe there will be a new car under their ballots."

"Rich?" Clapp asked. "But how did he make his money? Someone says he's connected to the mob."

Thrice turned to look at Clapp. She could never understand why he was on the panel. No doubt to represent the Alfred E. Newman crowd. "Are you serious, Seymour? What century are you living in? You can't do business in America without the mob. Who do you think takes your garbage? Your wife?"

Suppressing a smile, Foxglove glanced at his clipboard and stated, "He served in the military. Special Ops, but whatever he did is still classified."

"My man!" Thrice exclaimed.

"I also heard that his mother abandoned him when he was a child," Blessing said between clenched teeth. "And that he was raised in an orphanage."

"Why not also mention that he has black blood in him?" Thrice asked.

"You can't believe that story about Benjamin Franklin." Blessing shook his head in disbelief.

Foxglove put a finger to his earpiece to hear better. "Wait a minute." After a few seconds, Foxglove went on: "We just got word that an extensive genealogy search has revealed that what Savage claims is true. He does have a French background and an American background. Addie and Benjamin Franklin are his ancestors."

36

Myron Path stood across his *Newsmakers* panel in the MSBCS studio. "We understand that Governor Dickey is scheduled to announce her choice for Vice-President this afternoon."

Folly started his analysis. "We understand that she has decided to name her candidate early to get a jump on Carran and to take away some of the coverage on Savage."

Stillworth, who joined *Newsmakers* on occasion, offered, "I would bet she's going to pick someone no one is expecting."

"Like?" Path asked.

Folly, the newest member of the panel spoke up: "I agree with Lill. I think she's going to surprise us all. She needs a big kick right now, and the same old politicians just won't do anymore."

"None of the usual suspects," Path added.

"No," Folly piped up. "Polling shows that Savage is gaining the women's vote, at least most of them. So she has no choice but to solidify the white working man's vote."

The scene switched on MSBCS, as it did on every news station to Dickey at an outdoor rally being held in Battery Park in Lower Manhattan. There were thousands of people looking at a raised platform where Dickey and several of her campaign managers were standing.

"Thank you for coming," Dickey shouted into the microphone. That brought a round of cheers from her supporters. "You know this is the year for us. It is our time and we can do it."

The crowd started chanting, "YES WE CAN, YES WE CAN."

Dickey talked over the chant. "We need a Vice-President who is a real American."

The crowd took up a new cry. "YES WE DO, YES WE DO."

"We need a man," Dickey continued, "who knows how to defend when we need defense and how to push forward when we need offense."

"YES WE DO, YES WE DO," thousands roared. The sound reverberated throughout Lower Manhattan and up the canyons of Wall Street.

"So, let me introduce to you a proven leader on the field of battle—"

Although no name was mentioned, the crowd started applauding, cheering, and shouting wildly.

"… a man who is a proven winner."

"WINNER, WINNER," everyone started bellowing.

"… the first African-American NFL coach to win a Super Bowl, the former head coach of America's team, now to be part of a new American team, the future Vice-President of the United States, Bud Frostee Pippen."

Dickey's announcement was met with thunderous noise from the thousands at the rally.

Bud Frostee Pippen came on stage. He was a big man, six foot three, weighing in at 257 pounds, maybe 5 percent body fat. Standing next to Dickey he looked like a giant. He kissed Dickey on both cheeks and turned to the crowd who was now shouting his name, "FROSTEE, FROSTEE."

A man almost as big as Pippen had come on stage lugging a very large bucket. Pippen slipped his hand into the bucket and pulled out a football. He threw it out into the crowd.

90

That brought on wild cheering, people waving their hands, and yelling "ME, ME."

CASBC, like all the other channels, kept their cameras on Pippen throwing out the footballs. The voice of Igor Olshansky played over the sounds of the crowd. "So now we have it. Once again Governor Dickey has proved how savvy she is by picking Frostee Pippen as her running mate. Here's someone who will definitely appeal to white male voters."

Dickey stayed on the platform for over an hour. One bucket was replaced by the next. She smiled as she watched Pippen, trying to guess how many thousand votes would come with each football he threw out.

37

Carran's campaign headquarters occupied several large office suites in the Watergate complex. Its heart, which the campaign had dubbed "The War Room," was a thousand-square-foot room with windows looking out over Washington. Carran was standing at the window, sipping at the Manhattan he held in one hand. His back was to Oxenhammer, who was angrily pacing the floor.

Oxenhammer was more than agitated. He was livid. "I don't give a shit about qualifications. You can't govern until you're elected. And look at our numbers since Dickey picked Pippen. Shit—three days and you're already down ten points. Christ, Abel, we're neck and neck with that fuck Savage."

Carran slowly turned around. His face was ruddy, his eyes a bit glazed, a sure sign that he was on his third drink of the evening. "I want to shake things up." He walked toward the teakwood console where all the booze was standing. "Something… Sherman that will put us back in the game."

"A Hail Mary," they both heard. Carran thought Oxenhammer had said it. Oxenhammer thought Carran had said it. Neither had. I had!

"Yeah," Oxenhammer bumped his fists. "A Hail Mary. That's what we need."

Carran had reached the booze and started mixing himself another Manhattan. His back was to Oxenhammer.

Oxenhammer thought he had heard Carran say, "How 'bout Mary Dinswitt?"

Carran turned around. "Mary Dinswitt? That's not a bad idea. Huh. I met her once...I think."

Oxenhammer walked over to the bottles of booze. He poured himself a shot of Maker's Mark. Carran was now standing at the window, looking out as rain began to fall. He felt very peaceful. Something told him he was on the right path.

Both men heard, "She's perfect; not an intellectual, kind of a soccer mom type." Neither man had uttered a sound. Each thought the other had spoken. Of course, that was *me*.

"Mary Dinswitt," Carran repeated, rolling the name over in his head. "Oh, I remember—met her on a cruise with Republican governors. Has a bunch of kids. She's the Governor of Hawaii. She's a surfer."

Carran turned around to face Oxenhammer, who had come up behind him. "Perfect, Sherman. You're a genius."

Oxenhammer looked quizzically at Carran. Why was he a genius? It was Carran's own idea. But he said nothing. If Carran wanted to think of him as a genius, so be it.

"That's it!" Carran pinched Oxenhammer on the shoulder. "The surfer Mom every white guy wants to fuck."

38

As usual, Foxglove was standing in front of the huge monitor of *The Missing Point* program. Foxglove turned to look at the monitor and the camera moved with him.

The monitor showed a smiling Carran next to a perky, blonde Mary Dinswitt. Dinswitt was a good head shorter than Carran. He had his arm around her, and her sparkling blue eyes were looking up at him. It could have been a photo of father and daughter given the fact that she was twenty years younger than he. The monitor then ran a montage of Mary Dimwit, the Governor of Hawaii: campaigning, surfing, sailing, and taking care of her four children. She was smiling sweetly in every photo, her hair perfect, her makeup perfect... the all-American girl.

Foxglove turned back to look at the camera. "Once again Carran has proved himself a maverick in choosing Mary Dinswitt as his running mate. Up until now she has had very little presence on the national scene. She's been the Governor of Hawaii for three years. We know she surfs, she fishes, and being Hawaiian, we can assume she does luau.

The camera focused onto the smiling face of Dinswitt. Foxglove wanted to say *she's cute*. Instead, he said something that he had to apologize for later: "She'll certainly help Carran appeal to the lust in white male voters."

39

The opening shot on *The Nightly Show* opened with Golden seated at his desk arranging a stack of papers. After a moment, he looked up and appeared startled, as if he had just realized that he was on camera. He held up the papers and frowned. "So now we know Carran and Dickey will split the white male's vote—Carran taking the lusty men, Dickey the sports minded. So, tonight we are starting a new segment to educate the American public: *Christ or Antichrist, good or bad for America?*"

Golden disappeared and the pictures going out were clips of protesters facing one another all over the country. On one side people were carrying signs that read SAVAGE IS THE ANTICHRIST. They chanted, "Kill him, kill him," as they walked up and down the street. On the other side people were carrying signs that read SAVAGE IS THE ANTICHRIST. They chanted "Praise him, praise him," as they walked up and down the street.

The screen faded back to Golden. His face set, serious, with that little twinkle in his eyes. "Is Savage good or bad for America?" Golden asked. "Sarah Burnheart our chief woman-on-the-street reporter is out on the street asking the man on the street that question."

Sarah Burnheart appeared on the screen. She was a tall brunette in her early thirties. She was wearing a pantsuit with a white shirt that was unbuttoned too far down for network TV, but perfectly acceptable for cable. "We're in Midville Kansas," she announced, her deep voice carrying all the authority of her title, which was displayed on the screen: Our Senior Antichrist reporter. "Yes, Midville, Kansas, the psychological center of America… and I'm talking with Jack Maeserovsky."

The camera panned back and the screen showed Maeserovsky standing next to Burnheart. Measerovsky was a big man, carrying 240 pounds on a 6'4" frame. He was wearing worn Levis and a plain checkered sports shirt. His brown hair was rumpled and he had a two-day growth of beard.

Sarah turned the microphone toward him. "Jack… may I call you Jack?" she asked but didn't wait for the answer that never came. Maeserovsky just stared into the camera, like a deer caught in the headlights.

"Jack is a local electrician—"

"Well, I'm not really an electrician," Maeserovsky interrupted.

"But you are a man on the street?" Burnheart offered, not missing a beat.

Maeserovsky looked around, "I guess so."

"So what do you think about David Savage?" Burnheart asked. "Is he the Antichrist?"

"I don't know," Maeserovsky answered without any change of expression on his face.

"Do you think he's good for America?"

"I don't know."

Burnheart pulled the microphone away from Maeserovsky. The camera panned in on her and she filled the screen. "And there you have it. The man on the street speaking for all America."

40

Malcolm Ryan had been the host of *The Ryan Factor* for seven years. The show slanted every piece of news to Ryan's particular far right-wing point of view. He believed the liberal/socialist media had captured America, and Americans had to fight them with every means possible. A year before, he had run a series of programs about abortion clinics, suggesting Americans do something about it. Within a week, three had been firebombed and a woman had been crippled for life.

As always, Ryan was wearing a dark brown suit, white shirt, and dark tie. His dark brown hair was parted in the center. He was near-sighted and wore contact lenses for the correction. He was married, had a son and a daughter. His wife was an active member of her church. In every way, Ryan thought of himself as speaking for the average American, which included the fact that he was addicted to painkillers, even though he had no physical pain.

"Everyone is asking, 'Who is David Savage?'" Ryan stared hard at the camera. "I think that's been answered. He's not one of us." Ryan paused to let that sink in.

"So who is he?" Ryan asked, picking up both his arms, making his hands into pistols, and pointing his index fingers out at the millions who were watching him. "Does it matter who he is?" Again Ryan paused.

Then he pushed his thumbs down over his index fingers. "What we need is someone to take him out."

41

Governor Dickey had moved to New York City some thirty-two years before. She was born in Kentucky, got a scholarship to Columbia, and then went on to Yale Law School. She had worked for a short time as a corporate attorney for one of New York's prestigious law firms. Two senior partners made her an offer she couldn't refuse. She'd go into politics, work her way up from the bottom, and hopefully, eventually become President of the United States. In return, the two partners would set up an offshore corporation that she fully owned. Every year she received the same percentage of profits as if she had remained a partner. The money went from the offshore corporation to her numbered account in a Swiss bank.

It was an arrangement that had paid off handsomely for all concerned. Only the three principals knew about the arrangement, which was hidden in a series of "Russian Doll" type corporations. Dickey's husband knew nothing about it.

She had married Murray Fisher when she was just starting her political climb. Fisher was a local New York TV personality destined to become one of the first in-your-face, spare no humiliation, let's trash one another syndicated cable programs. He made a fortune when cable stations exponentially expanded and his show was syndicated. Fisher believed he was the one who had used his influence and money to move Dickey on her political career.

Dickey allowed him to think that. She was smart and strong-willed, but she knew never to play those cards up front. She and Fisher had two daughters who always campaigned with her. Dickey portrayed herself as "your average Mom." She was anything but.

The daughters were grown and out of the house, but Dickey and Fisher continued to live in their Upper East Side townhouse. They often watched television on the fourth floor that they had turned into an entertainment center.

They had been watching *The Ryan Factor*. When Fisher turned off the TV, he turned to his wife and said, "Well, you gotta say this about Savage."

Dickey glared at him.

Fisher saw the look. He knew that look—a storm's brewing. But he paid no attention. "Say what you want... he's certainly capturing people's imagination."

"What the fuck are you talking about?" She held back screaming. Lately Dickey couldn't stand Fisher. She knew the answer to the question she was continually asking herself: *why the fuck did I marry him?* Maybe she needed his connections and money as a cover when she had started out. Now? She didn't need him anymore. When she spoke, her voice was ice cold, scolding, "Don't you read the papers. He's even with me in the polls."

"You need some gimmick to humiliate him," Fisher said the first thing that came into his head, and humiliation, a gimmick for television, was always uppermost in his mind. For me, Fisher was an easy target.

"Well... you're the expert at that."

Fisher reached out to touch her arm, but she pulled further away on the sofa. "Hey, you're right about that. The show brings home the bacon, honey."

Dickey stared long and hard at her husband. What a fucking ninny, she thought. "I can't believe you. Savage is about to pass me in the polls, and all you think about is your show and who's the fucking daddy.

"Oh yeah. You want to know who's the daddy? You'll love this one. This Friday I'm gonna have a girl on who claims that Bruno Fuscati is the father of her child." Fisher sat back, smug.

"What?" Dickey cried. Instantly she knew what to do.

Dickey moved closer to Fisher on the sofa. Her hand reached down and unzipped his fly. A smile started across Fisher's face. Dickey's hand reached into his fly. Fisher's smile turned into a grimace.

"What are you doing?" he yelled and reached down to pull her hand out of his pants.

Dickey held on. "I'm checking to see if you have balls."

"You know I have balls."

Dickey leaned over. "Here's an idea," she said quietly, and whispered in Fisher's ear.

"How the hell am I going to do that?"

"Get one of your slimy investigators," Dickey said; and she let go of his testicles.

42

I finished my workout at the Lower Manhattan Athletic Club, showered, and brushed my teeth at a sink. When I finished, I didn't rinse off the toothbrush or throw it away as I normally do. Instead, I left it on the sink counter and walked into the dressing room.

A man wearing a custodian uniform came by the washstand. With his surgical gloves, he picked up the toothbrush and slipped it into a plastic bag.

43

The Friday edition of *The Murray Fisher Show, WHO'S YOUR DADDY?* had the largest viewing audience in the 2 to 3 o'clock time slot in the afternoon. Sitting in the guest chair was Alisha Bishop, holding her baby. She had smoked a joint before coming to the studio and was feeling good, high, and ready to rumble.

To the left of Bishop was one chair. It was reserved for the prospective daddy. Bishop had named Bruno Fuscati as the potential father. She was certain it was Bruno. He was not in the chair. Instead, there was an enlarged photo headshot of Bruno in the chair. With, of course, the tag line that he was the campaign manager for David Savage.

Fisher, wearing his casual Brooks Brothers trousers and tee-shirt, held a microphone as he walked across the stage. When the audience stopped clapping, he announced, "Today we have Alisha Bishop..."

The camera switched to Bishop, a grin on her face. This was a hoot, she thought. The pot had lifted her spirits and she felt good. She was a natural for TV. Maybe someone will see her and she'll get a contract. That'll show the son of a bitch.

When the camera was back on him, Fisher went on: " asking the question ..."

Fisher looked out at the audience, put the microphone out to them and they shouted as they had been instructed, "Who's your daddy?"

With that, Alisha did what she had been told: held her baby up in the air for all to see.

The audience broke into sustained applause that frightened the baby, who started crying. Alisha couldn't quiet the baby, and a member of the staff came out and put a pacifier in its mouth.

The focus was back on Fisher. "We asked Bruno Fuscati to come here, but he declined. He actually didn't decline. He never responded to our request."

A chorus of "boos" rang out from the audience.

Fisher knew he had a good crowd. They were reading their responses that were in front of them on large monitors.

"Yeah," Bishop blurted out. "It's just like him. But he's the father." She started giggling.

That brought sustained laughter and clapping from the audience.

"Well," Fisher said, as he moved around the stage to stand next to Bishop. "We have a little surprise. As always we took DNA samples from the prospective father." He took a long pause. "And we obtained another DNA sample that we were led to believe could be the father."

"What other guy?" Bishop shouted. "Bruno was the only guy I fucked before I had the baby."

"Well," Fisher moved to the center of the stage, looked out at the audience, smiled, and said, "DNA doesn't lie."

Fisher held the microphone out to the audience. "So?" Fisher asked the audience.

On cue, they shouted their response, "Who's your daddy?"

"The father..." Fisher took his time, garnering the anticipation, "is David Savage!"

"Who the fuck is David Savage?" Bishop screamed. "I never fucked him."

44

Foxglove had decided to dispense with his panel for today. He was sitting in a chair in the middle of the stage. "Every day there seems to be a new and strange twist to David Savage."

The camera panned from him, across a small, round table to a priest sitting in the chair on the other side.

"To discuss the latest twist… paternity," Foxglove paused and then made the introduction, "my guest, once again, is Father Francis Novak."

Novak looked directly into the camera, his facial expression tight, his eyes deep and opaque.

"Welcome, Father," Foxglove said.

Novak nodded his head, but the stern expression on his face remained solid. His thin lips parted slightly as he said, "Thank you."

"So," Foxglove asked, "is it humanly possible for David Savage to be the father when the young woman said she never slept with him."

"Of course," Novak said, spoken like the true didactic ideologue he was, dismissing any other possibility but his.

"How so?" Foxglove asked.

"It's quite simple." Novak turned away from Foxglove. The camera followed him. Novak looked straight ahead and when he saw the camera was focused on him, he said, "That would explain who David Savage is. Satan can do anything. He uses his surrogates to do his evil work."

"Are you saying that David Savage is Satan?"

"I'm only saying that that would explain how David Savage got the young lady pregnant."

45

Abe had changed since Evie had taken him to bed. That night he was so drunk, he couldn't remember exactly what had happened. The next morning when he woke up with Evie next to him, he had a sense of déjà vu. Something like this had happened before, but he couldn't quite pinpoint it. He wasn't sure if it happened to him or someone he knew.

Whatever it was, he felt different. He couldn't explain it. He explored his omnipotent mind, but didn't get an answer. He knew he had imposed certain limitations on himself when he took this human form. He accepted the fact that he just was different.

He looked at Evie's naked body. She was lying flat, face up on the bed, no covers on her, and he felt this new energy rushing through his body. He leaned over and caressed her body. It made him feel good. She opened her eyes, smiled at him, picked her arms up, and embraced him.

They made love that morning and, wide awake, Abe was like a tiger whose awareness of what he was had snapped into place and he reveled in it.

Now when he was in the deli, he thought about her all the time. He made sure to brush her, accidentally, several times each hour. Every touch sent a thrill through him. He loved it. Evie was the first woman he had ever had sex with and now he knew he was truly living as a man.

He changed the way he looked. He had his hair and beard trimmed. He bought new clothes, nothing extravagant: nice cotton slacks, conservative sports shirts, and comfortable shoes. He still wore his apron in the deli, but he constantly changed it for a clean one throughout the day. He no longer carried the white table napkin under his arm.

It was early evening and few customers were in the deli. Abe and I were seated at a table by the window. On the table were onion rings, French fries, chopped liver, herring, various breads, bagels, a bowl of whole pickles, a plate of sliced pickles, and several bottles of cream soda.

"You look good," I said to Abe, pushing the plate of onion rings toward him.

"Thanks," Abe said, and pushed the plate back toward me.

"What, you don't like onion rings anymore?"

"Well... I'm trying to lose weight. Cutting down on noshing."

"Because ...?" I asked.

"No because. I just am."

"Good, you look better this way."

Both of us turned our attention to the pickets in front of the deli. Abe had tried to get a restraining order to force them not to picket in front of his deli. I, of course, made sure no judge would grant the request. There were two groups facing one another, separated by police barricades. One group carried signs claiming I was the Antichrist and I should be killed. The other group carried signs claiming I was the Antichrist and should be praised.

Across the street, Latour walked back and forth and carried his own sign: THE DEVIL IS SAVAGE.

I turned back to the food on the table. I picked at the chopped chicken liver, put a large dab on the edge of a bagel, and started eating it. Abe watched me. His mouth was watering; he wanted a bite, but restrained himself.

"What's wrong?" I said, when I had swallowed my chicken liver. "You don't look too happy. Is it the pickets?"

"Nah," Abe said, moving one hand in the air as if brushing away flies. "They've been good for business. Every tourist wants to eat here and get my autograph."

"Which name are you using," I laughed. "Yahweh… the Lord… Jehovah?" I took another piece of bagel and slowly covered it with yellow deli mustard, then spread a glob of chicken liver on it, added several sliced pickles, and asked, "Allah?"

"It's you. They think I have some deep sinister connection to you."

I almost choked on the food. "That's a good one. You with a sinister connection to me."

"Well." Abe looked at me and held my gaze. I hadn't seen that look in many millennia. I think it was the bet about Hannibal. "I want to ask you a favor."

"Really?"

"Don't be a smart-ass."

"Okay. Shoot."

"I'm getting tired of the deli business. It's always the same, day in and day out."

I searched Abe's heart for a clue, but found nothing. "You're looking for an adventure?"

"I was thinking about you. You have an interesting life. Money gives you that life. If I had money like you, I could have an interesting life."

My God, I thought. He's asking me to corrupt him. The world has changed! "So."

"I didn't want to just have it. I want to earn it. I was thinking …"

I got the message. "Look, since I've been running, I've put all my holdings in a blind trust. I can't control what's done with it, but I can control who runs it."

Abe didn't wait for anything else. "I'll run it," he said, a broad smile on his face as he reached across the table and shook my hand.

I held Abe's hand. "Not so fast. I'll give you five million and see what you do with it."

Abe frowned. "What—you don't trust me?"

"You won't be Mister Nice Guy anymore?"

"I'll always be nice," Abe protested and withdrew his hand from mine.

I had a quizzical look on my face. "Well, Abe. You may be right, but you know what they say about money."

"Don't worry," Abe said, his face set, his belief assured that he would not be corrupted.

"Wanna'Bet?" I asked with a wink.

46

The Nightly Show opened, as usual, with Golden shuffling a stack of papers in front of him on his desk. He looked up, as if surprised, and asked, "So, do we know any more about David Savage? *Our Senior know-it-all reporter, Myron Smith investigates.*"

Smith was standing in front of a monitor showing a montage of pro-Antichrist and anti-Antichrist demonstrators. Smith, a tall, skinny man with a mustache and goatee, nodded and in a deep bass voice said, "Millions of people have been swept away by David Savage, believing he has all the answers, while an equal number of millions of people are frightened by David Savage and believe he is out to destroy America."

The next shot was Smith sitting in a well-appointed room with heavy drapes and book-lined walls. Sitting next to Smith was a stout fiftyish man with reddish, puffy cheeks and drooping eyelids. He was wearing a black clerical gown.

Smith made the introduction: "We are here with the Reverend Jones."

Jones had an involuntary coughing spell. When it was over, Smith asked him, "What do you think of David Savage?"

"This man is dangerous, evil!" Jones glared at the camera.

"What can he do to stop the wars? Can he end global meltdown? Can he feed the poor and save the children?"

"It is frightening because people have misplaced their trust. This man is not out to help them. If you look closely, you will see Savage is showing many of the characteristics of the beast.

"Right..." Then realizing what Jones had said, Smith exclaimed, "What?"

"I said," Jones's face got redder, angry... he wasn't sure what he was angry at, but he was angry and whenever he was angry, his face got redder. "He is exhibiting signs that he is the Antichrist."

"Come again?" Smith asked, as if bewildered.

"Savage is actually going to trick the world into worshipping him." Jones reached for a Bible that was on the table next to him. He held it up and shook it at the camera. "In the Book of Revelation it says that the Antichrist will destroy the world."

Smirking, Smith asked, "You're kidding? Huh?"

"I am not kidding, young man." Jones's voice was hard. "I am serious. The conditions are ripe. The Bible talks about the Antichrist arising from the sea..."

The screen showed a quick shot of Savage surfing.

Jones didn't see this and just went on, "Swift like a leopard, feet like a bear, and a mouth like a lion."

"You have proof of this, of course?" Smith asked.

"If you want empirical proof, no, I don't have it." Jones shook his head and clutched his Bible tighter. "But I am not going to retract what I said."

Smith screwed up his eyes at Jones, "Do you ever think about what you are saying?"

"Young man, I think very long and carefully about what I say."

"I don't think you think long enough," Smith said, and the picture faded into another church study with Smith sitting next to a gray-haired, smiling sixty-year-old man in a well-tailored suit.

"I am with Pastor William MacCallister Sidney."

Sidney nodded and shook Smith's hand.

Smith looked into the camera and said, "The accusation that Savage is here to destroy the world makes Reverend Jones angry."

Sidney reached out and put a hand on Smith's arm. "I wouldn't use the word angry. A man of God should never be angry."

Smith put his free hand over Sidney's hand on his arm. "But you are infuriated with Reverend Jones?"

"Not infuriated, but I do and do not agree with him," Sidney said, and moved his hand off Smith's arm.

"Say what?"

"I do believe Savage is the Antichrist, but he has not come to destroy the world."

"What has he come for?"

"To clear the path for the Second Coming of Christ."

Smith brought both fists up, "So he's one of the good guys?"

"Absolutely!" Sidney once again put a hand on Smith's arm to emphasize the point. "Look at him: He's suave, cool, the kind of guy you would feel comfortable having a latte with."

"Not to mention an arugula salad," Smith added as the screen went black.

47

The Ryan Factor was barely a half-minute old when Ryan, looking directly into the camera and the millions of people who watched his show every night, said, "Every one is asking who is David Savage. I think that's been answered. He's not one of us. So who is he? Does it matter who he is? What we need is someone to take him out."

* * *

At Carran's campaign headquarters at the Watergate, Carran turned off *The Ryan Factor* and walked over to his desk. He sat down, picked up his drink, took a sip, and looked at Oxenhammer, who was sitting across from him. "Christ, Sherman, look what's happened. Why did you send that kid out there with the fucking sign? Didn't you check him out?"

Oxenhammer threw his hands up in the air. "I never expected calling Savage the Devil would turn him into a celebrity."

"And Jones?" Carran asked. What did you expect from him?"

"I only mentioned it would be a good idea to preach against Savage. Christ, Abel, how did I know he would turn Savage into the Antichrist?"

"Jesus Christ!" Carran slammed his drink down on the table. The thin glass shattered, and booze and ice ran over the papers on his desk. Oxenhammer jumped up and started brushing the liquid off the papers. He made a mistake of standing too close to the desk and wound up brushing the liquid onto his pants.

* * *

Governor Dickey turned off *The Ryan Factor* and took the elevator in her townhouse to the ground floor, which had been turned into her command center. Hyman, who was sitting in the office, had just watched *The Ryan Factor*.

Dickey came up behind Hyman and angrily jabbed a finger into his back. "Damn it, Patch, what can we do?"

"About the protests?" Hyman turned to face Dickey.

"No!" she shouted, disbelief on her face. "About Savage."

Hyman had figured out what to do about Savage. It was something he had to keep close to his chest: the fewer who knew, the better for him. He waved a hand in front of Dickey. "Don't worry about him. He's a flash in the pan."

"A flash in the pan?" Dickey repeated with evident sarcasm. "The media has fallen in love with him. Shit, Patch, if he proves to be the Antichrist or even the Devil, they will love him even more."

"Don't worry," Patch said, laying a reassuring hand on Dickey's shoulder. "I'll take care of it."

48

Carran, Dickey, and I were standing at separate podiums on the stage in the auditorium at Marshall, a small college in the center of Rhode Island. Malcolm MacCambridge, one of the highly respected anchors for public radio was seated at a table facing us, his back to the audience. The audience consisted of a few hundred students, a few local residents, and a thousand representatives from the media.

"First of all," MacCambridge opened the proceedings, "I would like to thank you all for coming."

"My pleasure," I said, I jumping in before any of the others could speak.

"An honor to be here," Carran chimed in.

"I welcome the opportunity," added Dickey.

"Let me start with you, Mr. Savage," MacCambridge said.

"Shoot," I smiled and pointed my finger at the seated MacCambridge.

No! No tricks! I heard in my head.

I answered Abe without speaking: *What tricks? People want what they want.No tricks!* I heard Abe say once again. I smiled and looked out over the audience. As I expected, Latour was standing at the back of the auditorium holding his THE DEVIL IS SAVAGE sign.

The only way to give them what they need is to give them what they think they want and then flip-flop, was my unspoken answer to Abe.

49

Mary and Gladys Jones were watching the debate in their living room in Omaha. Mary and Gladys were twin sisters who had been born sixty-two years before and had spent their entire lives together.

"Doesn't he look like Michael?" Mary asked, her eyes glued to me.

"Michael?"

"Oh, you must remember, Gladys. Michael Wolfson, who lived down the block."

"Oh, that Michael," Gladys sounded surprised. "Your first boyfriend."

"My first love... I didn't want to marry him, and I've thought about him my whole life."

"Well dear," Gladys took hold of Mary's hand. "You can make up for that by voting for David Savage."

* * *

In the Marshall auditorium, MacCambridge's voice was loud and clear. "The question, Mr. Savage. We know how successful you have been in business, but how does that qualify you to handle national security issues?"

I stepped away from the podium and walked to the edge of the stage facing the audience. We had all agreed on the rules of the debate, one of which called for us to remain standing behind our respective podiums. I knew the others would follow the rules. I saw no need to do so. I knew MacCambridge would do nothing about it.

"I'm glad you asked that question, Malcolm. I have negotiated with the heads of twenty-five states. Some have been our traditional friends and some have been our enemies. I have sat with them and looked them in the eye, and in 142 negotiations, I have won all the terms that I have ever wanted."

* * *

At Casey's Sports Bar, across from Yankee Stadium, Gus, the bartender, was struggling with the TV's remote controls. No matter what he did, the only channel that worked was the one televising the debate.

"Damn," Gus shouted. "The fucking TV is stuck again."

* * *

"And how were you able to do that?" MacCambridge asked me.
"If I can borrow a term—" I went into my imitation of Don Corleone; I scratched my cheek with the back of my hand and said, "I made them an offer they couldn't refuse."

The audience in the hall broke into laughter and applauded wildly.

"I don't think the presidency is something to make fun of," Carran shouted from his place behind the podium.

"Well." I turned to face Carran. "Well, speaking of qualifications, I'd like to quote *Playboy* magazine." I turned around to face the audience. "Carran, a serial divorcee/adulterer has finally proven that marital fidelity has no bearing on someone's ability to do a job. In fact, paradoxically, it might be an indication of great leadership."

* * *

In Casey's Sports Bar, someone shouted, "Right on!" and many men started whistling and applauding.

117

* * *

Carran's face had flushed to a bright red. "Talk like that... I'm a different man now."

"Yes, you are," I said, as I walked back to his podium. "You've been consistent ever since you changed your mind."

The audience greeted that with howls of laughter.

"And you, Governor Dickey?" MacCambridge asked, swiveling in his chair to face Dickey. "What is your experience for dealing with world figures?"

Dickey had her serious face on. "You know, being the Governor of New York means that we're in New York and the headquarters of the United Nations. I've met with many world leaders when they have come to New York. I've had many over for tea."

* * *

Jackson, an ex-Marine cop, sitting at the bar at Casey's Sports Bar cupped his hands to his mouth and yelled, "Two fucking heroes."

Simmons, a house painter from Queens, was sitting next to him and threw one hand up in the air in disgust: "One's no better than the other. He's in bed with the fucking lobbyists, flying around in his fucking jet. I'm getting my fucking hours cut and he's talking about more tax cuts for his fucking rich friends."

Matthews, sitting at the far end of the bar, tossed out his comments. "She's no better. I don't trust that fucking smile. She smiles all the time. Fucking whores smile all the time. It's their come on."

Gus turned from looking at the TV and faced all the guys at the bar. "What about Savage? You know, he was once in here for a drink after a Yankees game."

"No shit," Jackson exclaimed.

"He's cool," offered Matthews.

Fisher, standing behind Jackson, said to no one in particular: "Who the fuck knows? You know they always say the Devil you know is better than the Devil you don't."

"Yeah," Gus shouted, pumping both fists in the air. "We know how shitty the Devils we know are, so maybe it's time for the Devil we don't know."

Gus turned back to look at the TV, and the picture was a shot of Latour standing at the back of the auditorium with his THE DEVIL IS SAVAGE sign.

50

Rikers Island is New York City's main jail complex. The 413-acre island sits in the East River between Queens and the Bronx. The fortress-like complex houses close to 14,000 inmates and 8,500 officers and civilian staff. The term Rikers carries a negative connotation, as the word itself has become a synonym for abuse and penal cruelty. No one goes there willingly.

The night after the debate at Marshall, a black S600 12-cylinder turbo Mercedes crossed onto Rikers Island and pulled up to the barrier at the edge of the East River. Hyman slowly got out of the car and walked toward a black S63 6.3-liter Mercedes fifty yards away. Oxenhammer saw him coming and got out of his car.

They did not shake hands when they met.

Hyman spoke in a whisper. "I think we both know what we have to do."

"He's a menace," Oxenhammer nodded his head.

"Have you set it up?" Hyman asked.

"No. I wanted to be sure you wanted to go through with it." Oxenhammer kept his voice low.

"Of course I do. We are doing this to save our system."

"Agreed."

"Do you know who you are going to use?" Hyman asked. He thought it was his idea—actually I put it in his head—but he didn't want any trail to him on this.

"Leave that to me." Oxenhammer knew exactly who he would use. "We are then agreed?"

"Agreed," Hyman said and extended his hand.

Oxenhammer shook his hand. Then both men turned away, walked back into their cars, and drove away.

51

Abe and I were standing at the urinals at Yankee Stadium. I was in my usual pinstripe suit. Abe had moved up in his sartorial quest. He was wearing lightweight linen pants, an open-at-the collar sports shirt, and a seersucker jacket.

"So?" I asked. "How do you like being a capitalist?"

"It's good. I've hired Izzy Pool to run the deli. I've taken an office in the Seagram Building, and I've started a hedge fund."

"Not bad," I patted Abe on the back. "Have you made any money yet?"

"I've gotten ten people to put in twenty million a piece."

Impressed, I asked, "How'd you do that?"

"I told them you were my partner."

"I know. They called me."

"And you said okay."

"And I said okay."

"But have you made any money yet?"

"Of course. I've taken my commission off the top."

"My man," I smiled. How quickly he learned.

The public address system came on. "Jackson's leading off the eighth for the Angels."

"I really miss the old place," I lamented

"I don't understand why they tore it down."

"Bigger and better bathroom facilities," I answered. "Just look around. Snazzy!"

"How long have we been going to the old stadium?"

"Once or twice every year since they built it."

"When was that?" Abe couldn't remember.

"Nineteen-twenty-three."

"Well, nothing lasts."

Just then, Jonathan Latour entered the men's room and approached us.

"Mr. Savage," Latour called out.

I slightly turned my head around to face Latour.

"You are the Devil," Latour said in a quiet voice. He then took several steps closer to me, raised his right arm. His hand held a 9.mm Glock. He aimed at my head and fired at point-blank range.

52

Foxglove was standing in the center of his set, holding a sheet of paper as the following text scrolled at the bottom of the screen. BREAKING NEWS: David Savage shot at Yankee Stadium.

Just in case anyone watching could not read, Foxglove announced: "We have breaking news. David Savage has been shot at Yankee Stadium. We have Cindy Witcher at the scene."

Cindy Wincher showed up on the full screen, a microphone in hand, in front of the men's room at Yankee Stadium. "We know that David Savage was shot tonight as he and his friend Abe Kandinsky were standing at the urinals inside this men's room, just behind me at Yankee Stadium." She turned and pointed to the entrance to the men's room.

"Anything else, Cindy?" Foxglove, off camera, asked.

"A moment ago, a black zipped-up body bag was removed from the men's room."

The picture switched back to the studio where Foxglove asked, "And was that David Savage?"

"The police are not saying." The screen once again filled with Witcher at Yankee Stadium. "The only thing we have heard is what David Savage's friend Abe Kandinsky, who was the only witness, told us."

"And what was that?" Foxglove asked.

"He said the man... we assume he means the shooter... came up to Savage and fired at point-blank range to his head—"

Witcher was cut off as the director of the program switched back to the studio. Speaking off screen, Foxglove said, "Just a minute Cindy. We have Colonel Mike Mitchell, a forensic expert with the National Guard on the phone."

A photo of Mitchell popped up on the screen. He was in the full uniform of the New York National Guard. His chest was covered with medals.

"Good evening Colonel," Foxglove said.

"Good evening," Mitchell replied, his voice deep and authoritative.

The screen was split in two: Foxglove on the right, the photo of Mitchell on the left. "Tell me, Colonel, what would be your opinion as to Savage surviving a point-blank shot to the head?"

"It would be a miracle for him to survive a point-blank shot to the head," Mitchell replied.

Foxglove said, "Thank you, Colonel." The photo of Mitchell disappeared off the screen, replaced by Cindy Witcher at Yankee Stadium.

"Cindy," Foxglove asked, "can we assume it is David Savage they carried out?"

"Yes," Cindy replied looking straight into the camera. "I think we can assume it was David Savage who they carried out."

"Has that been confirmed?" Foxglove asked.

"No. We are waiting for a police spokesman. We have been told one will be out in five minutes."

Foxglove was back live. "While we are waiting, we understand that Governor Dickey is about to make a statement."

Governor Dickey was standing in the street outside her townhouse. She had switched to a black pantsuit when she heard the news and knew the reporters were rushing over to get a statement from her. "It was with a saddened heart that I heard the news about David Savage. Although new to politics, he showed a willingness to learn and prove himself worthy of the high public office he was running for. As Governor of this great State of New York, I will do all in my power to find the perpetrator or perpetrators of this heinous crime and bring him—or her—or them—to justice."

She turned away and started walking toward Hyman, who was waiting at the entrance of the building. She never considered that the microphones were still live and could pick up everything she said: "I couldn't have planned it better myself."

It took all of Foxglove's professionalism to keep a straight face. He uttered a few sounds: "Ugh, ugh..." and then quickly said, "We found Abel Carran. He has a statement he wants to make."

The reporters had found Carran at his favorite seafood restaurant in Miami. Carran had gotten the news about Savage during the first course of the meal, but did nothing. By the time the stone crabs were on the table, the reporters were mobbing the front door of the restaurant, and Oxenhammer had convinced Carran he had to say something. Carran came out, still wearing his lobster bib.

"I am so saddened to learn about the untimely death of David Savage. He was a worthy opponent and he and his family—"

Oxenhammer whispered in his ear.

"I understand he has no family. But if he did, he and his family have my heartfelt tears, and I pray that he goes to hell where he belongs."

Again Oxenhammer whispered in his ear.

"To heaven where he belongs."

126

From the TCN studio, Foxglove announced, "We understand that the police are ready to make a statement."

The picture was back to Yankee Stadium. Captain Alphonse Mahoney was standing in front of the men's room door, surrounded by a group of shouting reporters and cameramen.

Witcher yelled, "Can you tell us what happened?"

Kennedy from MSBCS shouted, "Was Savage in the body bag?"

Austin from CASBC hollered, "Who's the shooter?"

Mahoney held up both his hands and waited till the shouting died down. He slowly looked around at all the reporters and then said, "Mr. Savage is okay."

Witcher asked, "And the shooter?"

"The shooter is dead," Mahoney calmly announced.

In unison, all the reporters shouted, "Who is he?"

"One of the problems," Mahoney started, "I would like to point out is that Mr. Savage refused our protection and the protection of the Secret Service, which he is entitled to as a candidate for President. As you may recall, Mr. Savage went to court to stop the Secret Service and us from protecting him."

"But what happened?" Kennedy asked.

"We heard he was shot at point-blank range," shouted Austin.

"That's correct," Mahoney shook his head in confirmation.

"But we heard there was only one shot," Witcher's voice cut through the shouting.

"That's correct," Mahoney answered matter-of-factly. "There was only one shot."

"What do you mean—only one shot?" Kennedy couldn't understand. "How'd the shooter get shot? Was there another shooter?"

"We don't think so." Mahoney hadn't moved since he started talking. Nor had he shown any facial expressions that would have hinted at the emotional content and contradiction of what he was saying. "Forensics will most likely verify our preliminary findings."

"What happened?" a voice cried out from the back of the pack.

"We believe there was only one shooter and only one shot."

"Wait a minute, Captain," Witcher inched closer to Mahoney. "You said there was one shooter, one bullet. So how did it happen?"

In disbelief, Kennedy shouted: "Don't tell me the shooter shot himself."

"Well... in a sense, yes."

"What?" came the collective cry. "Do you know who he is?" Everyone asked at once.

"Was he an American?"

"Was he a foreigner?"

"Actually, you have all seen him," Mahoney said and held up a small disk from the surveillance cameras in the men's room. "I'll let you see for yourself."

A monitor had been brought out, and Mahoney inserted the disk into it. After a moment, the monitor showed the inside of the men's room. There on the screen were Abe and I standing in front of two urinals. Suddenly Latour came into view talking, but there was no sound on the recording. The screen showed me shaking my head *yes*. Latour then took out a pistol and only inches away from me... fired. Mahoney stopped the disk.

"From here we have slowed it down to show you what happened," Mahoney said and restarted the disk.

In incredibly slow motion, the screen showed something grazing me, a flash as the bullet hit the top of the urinal, and then, it would appear, ricocheted back to the shooter, going through his eye and killing him instantly.

54

Foxglove anchored the late TCN show that evening. He wanted to be the one who would carry and explain the story of my survival. Foxglove was sitting in a chair surrounded by two men. "Everyone is abuzz with what happened earlier this evening at Yankee Stadium. As you recall, Colonel Mitchell said it would be a miracle for Savage to be alive if he were shot at point-blank range. To help us sort this all out, we have Rodney Basher, a former forensic specialist with the FBI, and Father Francis Novak. Thank you both for coming."

"It's my pleasure," Novak said, not cracking a smile or even softening up the cold, hard look on his face.

"Glad to be here," Basher said in his unmistakable Texas accent.

Foxglove turned to Novak. "So how would you explain this miracle?"

"First of all, I wouldn't call it a miracle. Only God, the Madonna, and the saints can perform miracles."

"So what would you call it?"

"An example of the Devil at work."

"You mean Savage deflected the bullet... like Superman or Wonder Woman?" They were the only two names Foxglove could think of who deflected bullets.

"Not like Superman or Wonder Woman," Novak scolded. "Like the Devil!"

"Is there anything you would like to add, Rodney... from a forensic point of view?"

"If Savage was shot at point-blank range and he survived as it appears from the tape, then I would say he's protected from up above by the Prince of Darkness."

"There you have it!" Novak pronounced. "David Savage is the Prince of Darkness."

55

Malcolm Ryan sat somberly behind his desk at *The Ryan Factor*. His hands were clasped together in front of him on the desk. He looked up, waited a few seconds, and then said, "I'm a God-fearing man, so I don't say this lightly about David Savage. Some have said he is not one of us... I agree. Some have said he is not a real American... I agree. I would go one step further... He is not one of us; he is not a real American. Not even a real man. He is the Devil!"

56

The Nightly Show opened, as always, with Golden shuffling and marking up a pile of papers on the top of his desk. As if suddenly realizing he was on the air, he looked up, smiled, and said, "Hi."

He put the papers down on his desk and said, "Follow me to the other camera."

He moved around to the right side of his desk where another camera was on him. "It's been a day since the shooting at the men's room in Yankee Stadium. The police say David Savage was not shot seriously. That he was only grazed by the bullet that was aimed point-blank at him."

Golden smirked as if doubting the veracity of what the police had to say. "That may be, but there has not been any sign of David Savage since yesterday. The police say that the shooter shot himself." Golden paused, scrunched up his lips. "Well, that too may be as the tape seems to prove. But there are many unanswered questions."

Golden moved around to the center of his desk. "Was the shooter taken out in a body bag? No one has seen the contents of the body bag. Is it possible," Golden put his pinky up to the corner of his lips in imitation of Mini Me, "as some have speculated, that this is a gigantic hoax?" Golden swiveled to the far end of his desk, "or maybe a cover-up is at play here?" Golden moved back to the center of his desk. "And what about this bit about David Savage being the Devil? Let's see if the pundits can shed any light of this."

The screen was divided into quarters; three were filled with the sets of three news cable shows. The fourth had a live shot of a Mister Softee truck.

Foxglove, in the TNC studio, was in the upper left quarter. "Well, we have no answers—only questions."

Path in the MSBCS studio was in the lower left quarter. "If he is the Devil, he is out to destroy this country."

Olshansky, over at Public Broadcasting was in the upper right quarter. "The questions everyone is asking have no answers."

Richter replaced Foxglove. "If he turns out to be the Devil, it will cause chaos."

Ripstein was where Path had been. "There are many questions being asked and many answers being given, but right now none of the answers answer the questions."

Clapp had replaced Olshansky. "If he proves to be the Devil, he will be bent on ripping apart the foundations of America that we know and grew up in."

Thrice appeared in one of the quarters. After shaking her hair around her head, she smiled at the camera and said, "I believe David Savage is an American man. He has said he will have an open and transparent administration. All he has to do is produce some evidence that he is or is not the Devil."

It was Hilderman's turn to make an appearance. "This guy, I believe is the Devil. This guy is a guy who has exposed himself over and over again. He's exposed himself as a guy who has a deep hatred for Americans, all Americans, not just white Christian Americans."

Folly had the last word: "His campaign is a Trojan Horse. Inside the horse are devils just like him, waiting to come out."

57

Three of the boxes disappeared, replaced by a split frame. A Mister Softee truck occupied the right half of the screen, and Golden was in the left half.

"So there you have it," Golden said in a deep voice, hoping to add gravitas to his statement. "What about Americans, the people they are talking about, the people they are talking for—what do they think? Let's go to our man in the street."

Smith, a regular on *The Nightly Show* was standing in front of the opened window of a Mister Softee truck. "We are here with our man on the street," Smith started, as the camera focused onto the window.

Standing inside the window was a fortyish man with long blond hair and a wispy blond mustache. He was wearing a Mister Softee uniform, with the name BOB written cross the left chest pocket.

"This is Bob," Smith said.

Bob sheepishly said, "Hi, yep, I'm Bob."

"So what do you recommend?" Smith asked.

'Well." Bob kept glancing from Smith to the camera that was pointed at him. Wow. He was excited. He was on television. Wait till the guys at the halfway house hear about this. "Our chocolate mocha-java jubilee with interlacing burnt banana caramel."

"Sounds right to me," Smith gestured with thumbs up. "I'll have one."

The camera stayed on Bob as he made the ice cream cone. He handed it to Smith who started licking it.

The camera went on Smith, who was getting the chocolate all over his lips and even his nose when he bit the cone from the side. "Hmmm, this is really good," he managed to get out.

Some chocolate dripped on Smith's white shirt. He paid it no mind. He thrust the microphone into the window. "So Bob, as the man on the street, what do you think?"

"About what?"

Smith took a few more licks at his cone and then asked, "Is David Savage the Devil?"

"I don't know."

"Do you believe in the Devil?" Smith asked. By now half his face was covered in chocolate.

"No," Bob said and, after thinking, added, "but I don't believe in God either."

Smith took the last bite of the cone, chewed it, swallowed it, and then asked, "Why not?"

Bob gave a little laugh. "Because if I believed in one, then I'd have to believe in the other."

"Well," Smith asked as he furiously wiped his face with a white paper napkin that was quickly disintegrating, "what if David Savage gets elected and gets us out of the mess we're in."

"Then I'll believe in him."

"And God?" Smith asked, throwing the soiled napkin into a bin next to him.

"Can't have one without the other."

58

The Pool Room was one of the power centers of New York City. The restaurant, designed by Philip Johnson, had been a landmark since its inception in 1959. Housed inside the iconic skyscraper designed by Mies van der Rohe, the restaurant was where the New York power elite congregated for lunch.

The Pool Room's twenty-foot ceiling and ever-moving aluminum blinds allowed soft light to filter down onto the dark wood that dominated the table and walls. Everything about it: the design, the atmosphere, and the service was designed to make it feel like an elite club, which it was. It got its name from the 14-foot square pool in the center of the room.

Abe and I were seated in one of the five "power" booths on the floor. I was dressed in my usual sartorial splendor. Abe surprised me. He was wearing a fine Italian wool, handmade suit, a beautiful Egyptian cotton shirt, and a fabulous tie that replicated Klimt's *The Kiss*. Most surprising were his soft leather loafers, which he wore without socks.

Another surprise was in store. In fact, the afternoon was full of surprises. When the owner of the restaurant, Mario Puchinelli, came over, Abe immediate ordered one of his rare Meursaults without consulting the wine list, which the sommelier had handed to me. As far as I knew Abe had never eaten here, let alone knew the wine list and then ordered my favorite Meursault.

When Puchinelli arrived with the wine, he looked at me first but then dutifully poured Abe a taste; Abe approved. Puchinelli poured tastes and we lifted our glasses. "L'chayim," we said simultaneously.

I tipped my glass at Abe and said, "So, I see you are getting into your new role?"

Abe didn't answer right away. He was working the wine around in his mouth so his tongue would capture the inherent flavors. Abe swallowed. "Yeah, only now can I really appreciate this wine."

"But you've been drinking it for years... years?" I laughed. "At least a century."

"Yeah, but I only drank it to keep up with you. I never allowed myself the pleasure of it."

"And now?"

"You know what's now. I'm a new man."

Before I could respond, Reuben Feinstein, the head of a multibillion-dollar hedge fund, came up to say hello. I extended my hand but didn't get up. "Nice to see you, Reuben," I said. "Do you know Abe Kandinsky?"

Feinstein turned to Abe and extended his hand. "Yes, in fact, I do. He's catering my son's wedding next week." Feinstein looked from Abe to me and then back to Abe. "Did you tell him?"

"No, not yet," Abe said, putting a hand up to stop any further discussion.

Feinstein got the gesture and left.

"So what are you doing with that schnoorer?"

"I didn't want to tell you till it was a done deal, but I'm getting him to put the money up for a new luxury building across from the deli."

"The one I wanted to tear down?"

Abe's reply was a sheepish grin.

"The building you worked so hard to save the tenants?"

Abe spread his hands apart. "I gave them an offer they couldn't refuse."

I burst out laughing. "You know if you keep at it, you could become worse than me."

"No," Abe protested. "Not worse, better at it."

The waiter delivered our lunch: we both had Dover sole. After we each took a bite, a sip of wine, Abe looked thoughtfully at me. "So you got them to think you are the Devil."

"Well, I am in a manner of speaking."

"And you think they will vote for you as the Devil?"

"Let's not talk about me. Let's talk about you."

Abe took a piece of sole, a sip of wine, looked at me, and said, "I don't know how to explain it."

"Let me explain it for you."

"Humm."

Puchinelli came by with a second bottle and offered us each a taste in a new glass. We both took a small taste. "Fabulous," I said. Abe had his taste but said nothing, put his glass on the table, and looked at me.

I took another sip of wine and then said, "You made man, so to speak, and then sat back content in your own little world. You couldn't—or wouldn't—see that Man made a fool of your prediction of his perfection?"

"I didn't think Man would make a fool of me," Abe said rather sheepishly.

"Of course not. It's your own fault. You didn't see because you didn't want to see. You kept saying in my image, in my image, and it was good."

"It *was* good," Abe said defensively

"What was so good about it? You thought you made Man in your image, and that he was perfect."

Abe pushed his plate away. He had lost his appetite. "And?"

139

"The schmuck believed you."

"Well, I used to feel connected even though I was alone."

"What are you talking about? You were never connected. You were alone, alone in your ego, of what you created, your rules of what should be."

"I never made them up. You know that."

"Well, that's the joke," I took a long sip of wine.

"What joke?"

"Your perfected being! Man made up all the rules and attributed them to you. They created your rules to suit themselves and you never said a word."

"What was I to say?"

"Tell them the truth."

"Which is?"

"Tell them they are on their own. Yes, you created Man, but you only created Man to see what he would do. That was the mistake."

"Mistake? What mistake?"

I stared hard at Abe. Oh God, I thought. It was like talking to a teenager. "Aren't you listening to me? When you said Man was perfect, those words—or rather the meaning, the energy behind the words—became part of Man's DNA, and since they were perfect, they could make up the rules."

"Whatever... Now I can't go back and don't know how to go forward."

"Forward with what?"

"With life..." he paused, and then added, "my life with Evie."

My answer was a broad grin. Abe leaned over to reach for the Meursault, but Puchinelli hovering nearby, beat him to it and expertly divided what was left into both our glasses.

"Ah, Evie. Enter the woman," I smiled. "You took a big bite out of her apple and now you can't go back. Before you were not engaged in the human experience. You sat on high and watched. Ah, but now. You've tasted woman. Woman connects you, grounds you, and puts you into the middle of life."

Abe had been listening. He understood, but didn't want to understand. Everything was changing too fast. He took a deep sigh and nodded at Punchinelli, who caught the gesture and went for another bottle of Meursault.

"Of course you understand," I said, patting Abe's hand that was on the table. "Sex... life is engagement with one another. That's why I am going to win the bet."

"Why?"

"Because I am engaged with Man and Man wants to be engaged. That's why he's always loved the Devil." I got up and walked around the table, stood next to Abe. "It's a Divine Comedy." I leaned down and kissed Abe on each cheek. "But you gotta learn the comedy is here, here on Earth, bubby."

59

I couldn't help thinking about how Abe had changed. I had expected it the minute he took the money and plunged into the world. Of course he was successful. He was no different than I. But I hadn't expected the extent to where Abe would go. Unforeseen consequences! I knew that one. I was a master of unforeseen consequences. What I had not foreseen were the changes in me. Nothing so overt or as obvious as with Abe, but a profound change, nevertheless.

Over lunch, I had come to realize that I no longer thought about the campaign to win the bet. I liked what I was doing. I wanted to help the people of the United States. As foolish as they were, I liked the Americans. Besides, I knew I was the best candidate to lead America into the 21st century.

60

On Wednesday, October 26, 1881, the most famous gunfight of the Old West took place at the O.K. Corral. The O.K. Corral, appropriately as it turned out, was in Tombstone, Arizona Territory, Cochise County. The gunfight lasted 30 seconds. Frank and Tom McLaury and Billy Clanton were killed; Morgan Earp, Virgil Earp, and Doc Holliday were wounded and survived. Wyatt escaped unharmed. The gunfight was a tribute to the fact that the frontier was an open range for outlaws, where the gun ruled.

Not much had changed over the century; at least not in many men's minds where the right to bear arms—and use them—was the sacred cow of American politics.

Afterwards, no one could explain why the Presidential debate was held in Tombstone, given its history and the growing vehemence toward my candidacy.

The town of Tombstone had erected a replica of the O.K. Corral and an amphitheater for the reenactment of the gunfight. It was their main, only attraction. There were billboards on the way to the town and in town advertising the time for the reenactment of the gunfight at the O.K. Corral. Now it was being used for a Presidential debate. Thousands of people lined both sides of the road leading to the amphitheater. There were signs that read "Kill the Devil" and signs that read "Love the Devil."

All the major networks, as well as many of the cable news networks were broadcasting the event. Cameras slowly panned along the road leading to the amphitheater. There were occasional glimpses of people carrying sidearms strapped to their legs and AR15 semi-automatics slung over their shoulders. Carrying weapons was legal in Arizona.

TCN broke away from Tombstone and had Foxglove in the studio. "Breaking News" was scrolling on the top and bottom of the screen. Foxglove's face was set, serious: "We will take you right back to the debate in a moment, but here is breaking news: OPEC has announced that due to the stalemated negotiations in the Middle East, they have decided that all OPEC members will, as of tomorrow morning, shut off all oil production. Within minutes of the announcement, a barrel of oil shot up one hundred dollars and is quickly approaching two hundred dollars a barrel. This will be a disaster for our economy and the way we live our lives. The price of gas is expected to go to six, seven, maybe even ten dollars a gallon. Now, back to the debate."

The open-air amphitheater had a raised stage that faced out onto a half circle of 750 seats. Ramses Mendelssohnn, the moderator of the debate, sat off to the side in a swivel chair so he could talk to the audience and us. There were three podiums evenly spaced in the middle of the stage behind which stood Carran on the left, Dickey on the right, and I in the middle.

Mendelssohnn was a rotund man in his mid-sixties. A full crop of gray hair, a full-face beard, and mustache. "Good evening from the Amphitheater at the O.K. Corral in Tombstone, Arizona," he said in his deep bass voice. "I welcome you to the Presidential debate between the Republican nominee Abel Carran—"

There was a chorus of cheers and boos.

"The Democratic nominee Governor Harriet Dickey—"

Another chorus of cheers and boos.

"And the Libertine nominee, David Savage—"

The audience erupted. Everyone stood up, screaming, yelling, cheering, booing, shouting "Kill him," mingled with cheers of "Love him."

Mendelssohn waved his hands in the air and asked for silence, but it was a full ten minutes before he could be heard. "I am Professor Ramses Mendelssohn from the University of Phoenix's local campus in Tucson Arizona. The questions have been prepared by me and not shared or cleared with anyone."

His announcement was greeted with a round of cheers and boos.

Mendelssohn held his hands up in the air, asking for silence. "The audience here in the amphitheater has promised to remain silent, no cheers, no applause, and no noise of any kind."

The audience responded with prolonged cheers and boos.

A man holding something in his right hand came running onto the stage. Several state troopers tackled him and started dragging him off the stage. Mendelssohn jumped out of his chair and ran over to the troopers. "Leave that man alone. He's my assistant."

The troopers weren't sure what to do. They looked at one another. "Here," Mendelssohn reached out and helped the man up. "What is it, Pedro?' Mendelssohn asked.

Pedro handed Mendelssohn the piece of paper he was clutching in his hand.

Mendelssohn read the paper as he slowly walked back to his chair. He sat down and read it a second time to be certain. He faced the audience and solemnly said, "Tonight's subject was to be about foreign policy and national security. Something momentous has happened."

There was a collective gasp from the audience. For a moment they were one.

"OPEC is stopping all production of crude oil as of tomorrow morning."

The announcement was met with a chorus of cheers and boos.

Mendelssohn swiveled in his chair and faced the three of us. "The price of oil is now over two hundred dollars a barrel. This is a crisis that threatens our economy and our very lives. I think a discussion of oil takes precedent."

"What?" Carran stammered. "You can't change the subject on me. I prepared for foreign policy."

Dickey smiled and slowly swung her arm out in an arc toward Carran. "There you go again. The President has to be prepared for any and every emergency at any time of the day or night. This is an emergency. Go right ahead, Professor Mendelssohn."

Mendelssohn looked at me. "Do you have an objection, Mr. Savage?"

"No, not at all." I looked every bit Presidential in my dark suit, white shirt, deep blue tie, American Flag pin in my label and, of course, a red, white and blue silk pocket handkerchief. "It is timely and oil is about foreign policy and national security."

"Quite right, Mr. Savage." Mendelssohn agreed. He turned to Carran. "So, Mister Carran, what would you do if you were President right now?"

Carran forgot to take the deep breath he had rehearsed with his coach. His face was flushed. He stared wide-eyed out at the audience. "Simple!" He thought for a moment and said the first things that came into his head, which of course came from me. "Rev up the bombers. Threaten every OPEC member with immediate military action unless they turned the spigot back on."

As could be expected, cheers and boos flowed from the audience.

"And you, Governor Dickey?" Mendelssohnn asked, turning his chair to face Dickey.

"First of all, we do not have the military capacity to threaten every OPEC member."

This prompted more boos than cheers from the audience.

Dickey smiled and waited till the audience was kind of quiet. "What we would need to do is sit down with the OPEC members and have a face-to-face conversation." I didn't have to put any thoughts into her head. She was always prone to say, "Let's talk it over."

Cheering and booing broke out in the audience and with it some shoving. The television cameras swung toward the audience, looking to capture the tumult they were expecting and even hoping for. They got a picture of a young couple. The mother was cuddling her baby; the father had his hands on top of the side arms he had strapped around his waist. TCN got the best picture of the night: an old lady in a wheelchair, wheeling herself toward the platform, an AR15 across her lap.

Mendelssohnn decided he could not control the crowd and turned his attention to me. "And you, Mr. Savage?"

I stepped forward from behind the podium and holding the microphone in my hand, I announced in a calm, deep, authoritative voice, "Allow me to introduce myself. I am the Devil and I am running for President of the United States."

The reaction from the crowd was instantaneous. Those that loved me were delirious with joy. Those that hated me were beside themselves with rage.

* * *

147

The scene was being played on the huge TCN studio monitor. Foxglove stepped in front of the monitor and said, "So there you have it."

"The chutzpah!" Hillerman broke in, his face red as a beet, "that he thinks he will get more votes running as the Devil."

"That's not the issue," Thrice snapped, shaking her long blonde hair.

Foxglove looked at her. "What issue?"

Thrice shook her head dismissively. "Not whether he is or is not the Devil."

"If that's not the issue, what is?" Foxglove asked, perplexed.

Thrice put on her most seductive smile. "We are a pragmatic people. The question is: is he good for America?"

61

"It no longer matters what OPEC does or doesn't do," I announced. My voice reverberated throughout the amphitheater. It held a pitch, a cord, a sound that got everyone to stop shoving, stop yelling, stop whatever they were doing. There was pin-drop silence.

"Actually, the timing is perfect," I paused and looked around the amphitheater. I had everyone's attention. "Yesterday I received a report from one of my geologists. I own thirteen thousand acres in the Dakotas. We've been drilling in a series of oil fields and we found an estimated reserve of some twelve billion barrels of oil under the land."

In the fifth row, Cabel McNeil jumped out of his seat. The cameras were on him and the AR15 slung over his shoulder. He started toward the stage. "We don't want the Devil's oil!" McNeil shouted. McNeil was thirty years old. He was a rodeo rider. He drove a big truck and had two enormous American flags flying from the rear. He had patriotic stickers plastered all over his truck. The only thing that was unpatriotic about McNeil was that he had never been in the armed forces, never been in combat, never put himself on the line for his country.

Two rows in front of him, Jackson Dawson stood up, unslung the AR15 he was carrying over his shoulder, waved it, and shouted, "We want your oil!" Dawson was forty-five. He drove a semi cross-country. He had been a member of the 82nd Airborne and a ranger. He had served three tours in Iraq and two in Afghanistan and been decorated for bravery four times, receiving a Purple Heart twice. He carried shrapnel in his left leg, which made him walk with a limp, and his left hand was bionic.

Instantly people begin shouting: "We don't want the Devil's oil" and "We want your oil." People began confronting one another. Men started jumping onto the stage. State troopers surrounded Dickey and Carran. I was left alone. (I guess they were expecting something like this, and it would appear they were instructed to leave me unprotected.)

McNeil had gotten on the stage. He held onto the sling of his AR15. One quick motion and he could level it. He walked menacingly toward me. Dawson had also jumped onto the stage and stood between McNeil and me; his AR15 hadn't moved, still slung over his shoulder. The troopers were silently sliding their side arms out of their holsters. Everyone else on the stage started backing away.

McNeil glared at Dawson. "You gonna defend that fucking asshole?"

"No, asshole," Dawson replied, calm as could be. "I'm gonna kill you."

"Says who?" McNeil spat and started to unsling his AR15.

"Says me!" Dawson never touched his AR15. Instead, he pulled out a Beretta 92FS and, without blinking, put three bullets into McNeil's heart.

62

The Nightly Show opened with a smirking Golden, shuffling his papers. When the applause died down, he stared hard at the camera. "Last night's debate turned into a brawl. They have suspended the next Presidential debate hoping things will cool down. I, for one, congratulate the discipline of the talk show hosts in trying to settle everyone down." He grinned. "No need to throw oil on the fire."

On his monitor, Golden played the opening of *The Ryan Faction Show*, Ryan at his table, grinning at the camera. "It was great last night," Ryan waxed enthusiastically. "People took up arms. They voted for the Second Amendment over the First Amendment. And God was on their side. Isn't that right, Father Novak?"

The camera panned to Father Novak sitting on the other side of Ryan's desk. "I believe so," Father Novak said. He made a little cough and then went on. "Although I don't presume to speak for God, we should not take oil from the Devil. It would be like selling our souls."

Golden was back on the screen. "Yes, he's right. He doesn't speak for God, but he certainly is right that we should not take oil from the Devil."

A frown crept across Golden's brow. He moved his chair to the side of the desk. The camera followed him. "By the way," Golden asked, "who *have* we been buying our oil from?"

63

Foxglove stood in front of the huge monitor that was at the back of his set. "The Presidential campaign has been turned upside down in the past twenty-four hours."

He stepped away from the monitor as the camera zoomed in to show two different groups of protesters across from my apartment building. Bunched in one area were people carrying signs "Kill the Devil," and people carrying posters showing me dressed like the Devil sitting on top of an oil rig, red blood flowing from the rig and the words "We don't want the Devil's oil." People waving American flags were interspersed with the group.

Separated by a police barrier were people carrying signs "We love the Devil," and people carrying posters showing me dressed as Uncle Sam sitting on top of an oil rig, black crude flowing from the rig and the words "We want the Devil's oil." People waving American flags were interspersed with the group.

Foxglove stepped back in front of the monitor as the camera pulled away. "Right now it appears that the campaign is all about David Savage. The other two candidates have been pushed into the background. Because of the violence that attended the last Presidential debate, the Commission on Presidential Debates has suspended the remaining two debates until after the Vice-Presidential debate. That debate will take place in two days, and we will broadcast it live on this network."

64

Abe was taking several practice swings before stepping up to the first tee. He was wearing a Polo sports shirt and slacks and Footjoy golf shoes. He was wearing his beard cut close to his face. He also had his hair-stylist sprinkle black dye to give his hair, beard, and mustache a salt-and-pepper look.

As he approached the ball on the tee, he turned to me. "I'm going to play my age."

"And how many millenniums would that be?"

"My age now, and I'm feeling younger and younger every day." He pounded his now flat belly. It made a hollow sound.

"Yes, very nice," I agreed. "I've also noticed you rolled the clock back with your hair."

Abe had used "product" to keep his hair flat on his head. He patted the starchy surface. "Nice, huh?"

"If you are going for that Pacino, DeNiro, Godfather, Goodfellow button-man look."

"What do you think of the outfit?" Abe pirouetted around in a small circle, swinging the golf club over his head.

"Not bad."

"Well, I'm taking your advice. I am learning about being a man."

"Don't forget. It took a woman."

"Speaking of that—" Abe walked away from the tee and approached me. I was standing on the car path. Abe looked at the four players a bit down the path impatiently waiting to tee off after us. Abe whispered, "We have to revise our agreement."

"Which agreement?"

"How long we are going to stay in these roles."

"I suspect you want to stay longer."

"I'm no longer like I was, and I'm getting to like who I am and what I can do."

"Nothing corrupts like power, and nothing comes close to absolute power."

Abe walked back to the tee, took a few practice swings, approached the ball, and shouted over to me, "So how much a hole... a thousand... two?"

"Are you kidding?" I was happy to bet any amount. It was only play money—all our money was play money. "This will be like taking candy from a baby. You've never played golf."

"Candy from a baby?" Abe stood behind the ball looking down the fairway toward the green, some three hundred and ten yards away. Abe calculated what he had to do and walked back to the ball, took his stance, and announced, "Watch me and it's two thousand a hole."

Abe's eyes stayed glued to the golf ball and with a perfect swing hit the ball three hundred twenty yards onto the green. The ball landed softly on the back of the green and slowly started spinning back some eighteen feet to fall into the cup.

It took us a little less than two hours to play the full eighteen holes. Abe won thirteen. We were sitting on the veranda of the clubhouse looking out over the course. When a waiter came up to us, I said, "I'll have a Kendricks Martini straight up and very dry. "

"I'll have a Gray Goose," Abe said, "straight up and very dry, two olives and a twist."

"So you're drinking now?"

"I am."

"And you won a lot of money."

"That'll teach you to bet," Abe laughed.

"Given your skills and what you did today, I would say you are up to the Devil's tricks."

"Look who's talking? I won fair and square," Abe said indignantly.

"You mean you didn't do anything I wouldn't do."

The martinis arrived and we clinked glasses, said a simultaneous "L'chayim," and both sat back in our chairs sipping our martinis.

"So, Abe, you really want to stay longer?"

"I do."

I screwed my eyes onto Abe's face. "Because of Evie?"

"Because of a lot of things," Abe answered.

65

I gave Abe a lift back to the city in my limo. As soon as Abe sat down, he asked, "Anything to drink in here?"

I reached out for the bottle of champagne, "You really have changed."

Abe held his glass out, "More than you can imagine."

The limo stopped in front of a luxury apartment on East End Avenue. The building occupied an entire block, from East End Avenue to the East River. Abe got out and went into the building. He had recently bought the penthouse floor and had it totally redecorated.

The limo continued on.

I took out my cell phone and punched in a number.

The receptionist at the Union Swiss Bank of Basil answered the call. She spoke in German. "Union Swiss Bank of Basil."

I answered in German. "Herr Docktor Dieter Obermeier."

"Who is calling please?" she asked.

"Max von Beckendorf."

"Yawohl, Herr von Beckendorf."

Obermeier's office had dark wooden paneling, heavy leather furniture, and thick old drapes drawn tight so no sunlight ever entered the room. There was a small lamp on Obermeier's enormous heavy oak desk. He stood between his chair and his desk holding onto the phone. "Good to hear from you, Herr von Beckendorf."

"Is everything ready?" I asked in perfect German.

"Everything is ready, Herr von Beckendorf. We have reached an agreement as you proposed. We are just awaiting your approval."

"You may proceed," I said, smiled, sat back in the limo and took a sip of champagne.

66

It was halfway through the morning panel show at MSBCS when Path heard the news in his earpiece. He broke off the conversation with his panelists and announced, "We have breaking news. Union Swiss Bank of Basil, known as USBB, has agreed, as part of a U.S.-Swiss tax-evasion settlement, to produce at least ten thousand names of Americans who have hidden money overseas to avoid paying millions of dollar of tax."

At TCN, Foxglove was announcing, "We have a TCN exclusive. In an agreement reached earlier today, Swiss banks are turning over the names and account numbers of Americans who have hidden money in Switzerland banks to avoid paying taxes."

Not to be outdone, Olshansky at BBTTC excitedly came onscreen. "We have exclusive late-breaking news. One of the names the Union Swiss Bank of Basil handed over to the IRS is Harriet Dickey, the Democratic candidate for President of the United States."

"That's not so unusual," Richter chimed in. He was always promoting more wealth for the rich, the more hidden from the IRS, the better. "It's legal."

"Not really." Olshansky glared at Richter. He hated it when Richter upstaged him on his own show. He sneered at Richter and then turned back to the camera.

"Big deal," Richter snarled and threw his hands in the air. "So what are we talking about, a few million dollars?"

"No," Olshansky said calmly, "it's more like two hundred and seventy-three million. And," Olshansky could hardly control his glee, "she earned it all the time she was a government official... it was all a payoff."

67

Foxglove was holding his clipboard from which he never read. "The Vice-Presidential debates, scheduled to take place tomorrow evening, might not happen. Governor Dickey has just made this statement." The screen was filled with Dickey. Next to her was her visibly angry husband and their two twenty-something daughters. They were standing in front of their Manhattan townhouse.

Dickey, holding back tears, was reading from a piece of paper. "The vile unscrupulous reporting from a biased media about my finances has taken a terrible toll on my husband and my daughters. I love my country, but my first responsibility is to my husband and our family. Because of that, I have regrettably withdrawn from the Presidential race. I also realize that we are very close to the election. Considering that, I have asked the DNC to elevate Bud Pippen to the Presidential nomination, and they have agreed to do so under the rules of our nominating procedure."

The family faded from the screen, and the camera was back at the TCN studio and Foxglove, who asked, "The question now is can the debate tomorrow go on, since Bud Pippen is no longer the Vice-Presidential candidate?"

Foxglove turned to his panel, but before anyone could answer, Foxglove lifted one hand to stop them and put a finger from the other hand up to his earpiece. A look of bewilderment crossed his face as he spoke. "We have just been informed that the Commission on Presidential Debates has consulted all parties, and all have agreed that the debate will go on as scheduled tomorrow evening. We have just reached Abel Carran."

Carran appeared on the monitor. He was standing outside the Watergate Complex in Washington, D.C.

"Mister Carran," Foxglove asked, "do you have any comments about Dickey's withdrawing and that Bud Pippen will be the Democrat candidate."

Carran had already held a strategy session with the campaign team. They were elated. Carran would make mincemeat out of Frostee Pippen.

Carran looked at the camera and said, "I am saddened to hear that Governor Dickey had to resign, but I do understand this concern for her family and I applaud her on that."

Off screen, Foxglove asked, "And as for Bud Pippen?"

"I'm sure he will be a worthy opponent."

68

Barricades were set up in front of the auditorium of Back Bay College in South Boston. Behind one set of barricades, people were waving signs: "We don't want the Devil's oil." The barricades across from them held back people waving signs: "Give the Devil his due—Vote for Savage."

In the BBTTC studio, Olshansky was saying, "This is one of the most unusual evenings in American politics. One of the Vice-Presidential candidates is now the Presidential candidate, and while it is supposed to be a three-way debate among three political parties and their philosophy, the nation has polarized for and against David Savage, whether he is the Devil and if he is, is that good for America?"

Abe and I were watching the broadcast sitting in Abe's new apartment, eating deli food, and drinking champagne.

This was the first I had seen of Abe's new apartment. I had walked around admiring the art and furniture and, of course, the river view. "Well, I'm glad you have gotten into this." I lifted a glass to Abe.

Abe clinked glasses. "You know it's funny. From high above I made up all those rules without understanding the collateral damage they would do. It's good to be a real man here now and begin to have an understanding of how Man has interpreted everything."

"Wrong!" I added. "Misinterpreted."

"Mea culpa," Abe acknowledged. "I shouldn't have been such an ideologue."

I slapped Abe on the thigh. "Good. You're learning. Now let's watch this." We turned to the TV and the debate.

Seated on the stage at the Back Bay College auditorium were Dinswitt, Pippen, Williams, and August Augerstein.

Augerstein saw the signal from the director and started talking. "Good evening from Back Bay College. I am August Augerstein, Professor of linguistic phonetics and faculty adviser to the dialectic debating society of Back Bay College. Welcome to the first and only Vice-Presidential debate between the Republican nominee Mary Dinswitt, the Democratic nominee, Bud Pippen, and Rue Williams, the Libertine nominee. As you must all know by now, Bud Pippen is now the Presidential nominee, but all the parties have decided to engage in this debate as planned. Straws were drawn to determine who would go first, and Governor Dinswitt drew the short straw."

Augerstein turned to face Dinswsitt. "Governor Dinswitt, why do you want to be Vice-President?"

"Thank you, Dr. Augerstein." Dinswitt lit up the screen with her smile. She had a good smile—not great, but good. It had gotten her to be a cheerleader, a wife, a state representative, and governor. Now she fully expected that smile to win her the Vice-Presidency. She looked right into the camera, her smile fixed in place. "I appreciate my opportunity of riding a barrel here," she paused. "That's a surfing term," she giggled. "I appreciate being here." She stretched out one arm, sweeping it across the audience, fingers in the Hawaiian *shaka* greeting. "Being here with real Americans." A cheer went up from some in the audience. "Being here, speaking with real Americans." Another cheer went up, not as enthusiastic as the first.

163

"The America I know," Dinswitt started. "God Bless America, land that I love." She paused, flashed her smile "… to crown thy good with brotherhood from sea to shining sea." Her rendition was greeted with cheers, hoots, and whistles.

She stopped singing and said, "We are at the sea where America started, and I come from the sea at the other end of America."

She looked around, first at Pippen, and then wagged her finger at Williams. "The America I know isn't a closeout, we're not in the impact zone; we need to cut back and make sure the Devil isn't President."

A few people raised signs and were immediately escorted out.

"Running for President is a rip." There were some desultory cheers and not a few gasps at her mis-mentioning the office she was running for. She smiled. "Hey, that's great. Some of you East Coasters know the language I speak." A few cheered, but most of the adults and the students in the audience didn't have a clue what she meant. "My stance is what America is all about—limitless possibilities, keep that crest up and make sure we don't crumble." Dinswitt waggled her *shaka* hand in the air. "Let's go bombin' America!"

Her exclamation was met with a few half-hearted cheers from the audience.

"Thank you, Governor," Augerstein said stiffly. He shifted in his chair and turned to Pippen. "Mr. Pippen, my original question was why do you want to be Vice-President, but now I have rephrased it to why do you want to be President?"

"Call me Frostee, Auggie." The rules were that each candidate would sit in the chair. Pippen's rule was that rules were meant to be broken. He jumped out of his chair and paced the front edge of the stage, talking out to the audience. "I'm running for President. That means I'm the quarterback. I know our playbook. I know we have a balanced line, and we will never be blind-sided."

A few people raise signs and were immediately escorted out.

Pippen continued to pace the edge of the stage. "The country has been in a false start." That brought a few whistles from the audience. "No one's been umping. No one's been making the right calls. Team America needs a new playbook."

More whistles.

"On defense, we're gonna blitz the rich and powerful who have bootlegged this country from us. On offense," Pippen was gesturing wildly with both hands in the air, "with me as your quarterback we will run and pass. We'll call audibles and keep our men in motion." Pippen paced the edge of the stage, stopped and spread his legs into a squat, stared out at the audience, held both arms straight out, and shouted, "We'll pitch out, have power sweeps, screens and slants until we cross the goal line and put up the extra point."

That brought most of the men in the auditorium to their feet, cheering. Post-debate analysis couldn't decide if the men were standing and cheering because they believed what Pippen said or because of the way he said it. All the talking heads agreed he was speaking a language men did understand.

Augerstein turned and faced Rue Williams. "And Ms. Williams?"

Williams got out of her chair, walked to the edge of the stage, waved at the audience. "Hi everyone." Everyone in the auditorium was on their feet, wildly cheering.

69

At the same time the debate was going on, Hyman and Oxenhammer were standing in a corner of a deserted warehouse in the South Bronx. Oxenhammer was fidgety and kept moving back and forth. He wasn't comfortable being in the South Bronx and alone with Hyman, who couldn't do anything if some gangs attacked them. "Are you sure he's going to show?" Oxenhammer asked. It was the third time he had asked the same question.

Hyman replied with the same answer he had offered before: "He'll be here."

No sooner had Hyman said that, than Moise Reiner emerged from behind a pillar.

Oxenhammer jumped. "Shit! You scared the shit out of me."

"That's why you're hiring me." Reiner spoke English with an Israeli accent. He was of medium height, wide at the shoulders. He stood flatfoot and looked straight at Oxenhammer. No smiles. His eyes bored right through the man.

Hyman walked over to Reiner. They didn't shake hands. Hyman gave Reiner a plain manila envelope. "Here's half. The rest you get when the job is completed."

Reiner slipped the envelope into an inside pocket of his black leather jacket. "The press pass," he asked looking from Hyman to Oxenhammer.

Oxenhammer handed him the press pass.

Reiner put the pass in an outside pocket of his jacket. His hand withdrew a roll of antacid tablets. He slowly ripped open an end and popped a few in his mouth.

"What's wrong?" Oxenhammer asked. "Are you not well?"

Reiner thumped his chest with his fist. "Indigestion."

"Good," Hyman said. "Don't get sick on us."

Reiner turned and disappeared into the dark vastness of the warehouse.

Oxenhammer and Hyman started walking. Oxenhammer forcefully took hold of Hyman's arm. "Are you sure about him?"

Hyman moved his arm in the air, dislodging Oxenhammer's hand. "Best hit man the Mossad ever had."

70

Williams stood still in the center of the stage until the applause died down. "How ya'll feeling?" she asked waving her arms in the air.

Almost everyone in the audience was back on their feet yelling hysterically.

"That's good," Williams shouted back at them.

One woman in the audience shouted, "We love you, Rue."

The audience took up the cheer: "We love you, Rue. We love you, Rue."

* * *

In a poorly lit, trash-strewn living room, Bill Wrightson was watching the *The Ryan Factor* on his old television set. Wrightson was dressed in combat boots and camouflage fatigues. He was sitting in his battered barcalounger guzzling beer from a can.

On the TV Ryan was holding up a picture of me and Williams.

"I keep saying, they are not one of us." It was a line Ryan had been hammering out ever since the nomination.

"Fucking A," Wrightson shouted and swung out his beer can, saluting Ryan. Beer spilled all over Wrightson's pants, but he paid it no mind.

Ryan looked straight at the camera. "So whose gonna take them out?"

Wrightson jumped out of his barcalounger. "I will man. Me and my buddies. We'll do it. Get rid of that fucking nigger and her fuckin Jew boy friend running for President."

Wrightson took a swig from the beer can, but it was empty. He crushed it with his hands and threw it over his shoulder. It fell on the seat of the barcalounger. He kicked debris out of his way as he walked to the refrigerator that was in a corner of the living room. He pulled out another beer. He opened the beer as he walked back toward his barcalounger. A picture on the wall caught his eye. It was Adolph Hitler. He stopped and saluted his Führer with his can of beer. "I'm gonna do it for you, man." He emptied the can of beer in one long swig. "Yeah," he said. "That's what I'm gonna do." He crushed the can in his hands and threw it into the living room.

71

The audience was cheering wildly in the auditorium of Back Bay College. Augerstein had asked them to be quiet and sit down, but they paid no attention to him.

Williams finally held both hands up in the air. "Please. Thank you. Now, will everyone sit down?"

Slowly the audience quieted down and took their seats.

Williams walked to the front of the stage. "You are all so close to my heart. The vice Presidency is close to my heart because we no longer want to be shoved or pushed into things we don't want to do."

That brought sustained cheers from the women in the audience.

"We want our freedom, our ability to be who we are. Remember... anything is possible." That brought more cheering.

"And we can win this campaign with good manners. Isn't it more fun to have good manners?"

* * *

Ali Akbar and four other men were sitting on the floor of an empty apartment in Brooklyn. The only furniture in the room was a television tuned to the debate. The four men looked from the television to Ali Akbar.

Akbar spoke to them in Arabic. "I know we have trained and have been waiting. The Lord Mohammed, Blessing and Peace be upon His name, has spoken to me. There..." Akbar pointed to the television. "There are the American Devils."

Akbar and the four men rose as one and declared a jihad, shouting at the television.

7 2

"All we need—" Williams had cast a spell over her audience, as she always did. "All we need is to speak manners and good will into existence." She paused, knew they were with her, and went on, "Pray it into existence. That's the power we have within us." She stood there, her arms stretched out, asking her audience to fall into them.

They did: cheering whistling, applauding, and, of course, many crying, "We love you, Rue!"

Williams allowed them to carry on for a few moments and then asked them to sit and be quiet. They did.

"As you all know, David Savage and I are going to hold our closing rally on October 31... Halloween at the Hollywood Bowl in Los Angeles. I want everyone here in the audience to know that as they leave here tonight, they will be handed an envelope. Five hundred of those envelopes will contain a coupon for two round-trip flights to Los Angeles, a hotel stay of five days, and two VIP Reserved tickets to the rally."

The audience erupted with wild applause and shouting.

When they stopped, Williams announced, "For the rest of you out there, the rally will be free and because it's Halloween, you will only be admitted if you are in costume."

73

Billy Madison, the producer of TCN's special events, sat in TCN's mobile trailer outside the Hollywood Bowl. He was looking at six monitors, scanning the activities outside and inside the bowl. He had assigned six cameramen to the event. Half were behind stationary cameras. Two were walking around with mobile cameras. The sixth camera was in the blimp slowly circling overhead. Madison pressed camera 1. The scene going out over the airwaves was a panoramic view of the Los Angeles area: the downtown skyscrapers, the Pacific Ocean, the San Gabriel Mountains. Madison stayed with camera 1 as it zoomed down into the Hollywood Bowl. Thousands of people were streaming in, everyone dressed in costumes. A band on stage was playing Dixieland Jazz.

Madison switched to camera 2, following Foxglove as he approached a group of angels.

Madison turned to Ryan Jackson, his assistant director. "Those guys sure as hell don't look like angels."

"Why," Jackson smirked, "just because they are big, unshaven, and rough looking?"

"Yeah and look at their boots," Madison said.

"Combat boots?"

Foxglove had reached the angels and extended his microphone toward the biggest one. "Excuse, me. Can you tell me why you are here?"

Wrightson stopped, looked Foxglove up and down, leaned toward the microphone and with a gnarly voice said, "Fuck off, faggot." Wrightson and his buddies stormed off through the entrance.

Foxglove turned and looked at the camera. "Not real angels, I guess."

Madison was still laughing when Foxglove approached a couple dressed as The Honeymooners.

"Excuse me," Foxglove held the microphone close to his chest, waiting to see what these two were like before giving them airtime. "Can I ask you why you are here?"

"This is a gas, man," Jackie Gleason said and did a little Jackie Gleason dance step. "I love that guy."

"Which guy?" Foxglove asked.

"Savage."

"Why?"

"Are you kidding? How often do you get a chance to give the Devil his due?" The phrase had gone viral over the internet and was on everyone's lips.

"Do you think Savage is the Devil?" Foxglove asked"

"You gotta be kidding, right? He's a politician. They're all devils."

"Why would you vote for Savage then? What makes him so special?"

"Jesus Christ," Jackie Gleason exclaimed. "You're on television. You're the media. Don't you understand? He's the first one to admit that he is the Devil."

A group of men dressed as Hassidim hurried past Foxglove and The Honeymooners. One of them bumped into Jackie Gleason.

"Hey," Jackie Gleason shouted. "Watch it buddy."

One of the Hassidim mumbled "go fuck yourself asshole," in Arabic.

Suddenly there was a roar from inside the Hollywood Bowl. Everyone was shouting, "He's coming, he's coming."

I, dressed like the Devil, and Rue Williams, dressed like Marie Antoinette, walked onto the stage. Many devils and many Antoinettes accompanied us. Our entourage were members of a select security team I had put together. The crowd roared its approval as Williams and I paced the front of the stage, our arms up, signaling victory.

Reiner, with his press pass around his neck, slowly made his way through the crowd to a television tower. He was not in costume, just jeans and a black tee-shirt. He was carrying a large black leather workout bag. When he got to the tower he started climbing up. He had arranged for a crew to construct the tower. It was supposedly to be used by Independent Euro news.

I took the microphone, moved to the edge of the stage, and shouted, "Allow me to introduce myself..."

The crowd knew where to go from there. They shouted as if rehearsed. Well... I was pushing their buttons: "I am the Devil and I am running for President of the United States."

The roars were ongoing until I raised my hands for silence and got it. "Welcome to the greatest Halloween party in the world."

William Melendez, a TCN cameraman in tower 4 panned the crowd and moved up the tower directly across from him.

In the TCN trailer, Madison was watching his monitors. "William, what the fuck are you doing?" he spoke through his headset.

"I'm curious to see who's in the tower."

"I was told it's some guy making a documentary for European television."

"Oh yeah," Melendez said. "I've done some work with them. Just a second. Let me see if I know the guy."

"Fuck!" Melendez shouted.

Madison's monitor # 4 showed Reiner as he was securing his rifle around his shoulder and hand. It was aimed at the platform. Madison put that picture out over the network. He then called the police number he had been given for an emergency.

74

Rue and I, holding hands, walked back and forth across the stage several times. Then I handed the microphone to Rue and, in a powerful happy voice, she announced: "Come on everyone, let's party."

The band broke into heavy metal music.

* * *

Abe and Evie were hosting their own Halloween party in his penthouse. It was a black tie event. There were thirty-five people, all new friends whose combined wealth was more than the bottom forty percent of all Americans. It was champagne, caviar, and *foie gras*. Large flat-screen televisions sets had been placed around the apartment so everyone could watch my Halloween party rally.

No one had been paying much attention to the television until the picture of Reiner with the rifle came on. Now everyone was scrambling to get as close as they could to the monitors.

"Oh my God," Evie screamed as she grabbed hold of Abe's arm. "He's going to kill him!"

"No, he's not," was all that Abe said as a smirk crept across his face.

* * *

The picture that went out to all America was Reiner sighting through his scope. There was a pronounced quiver in his face. He reached into his pocket and took out a roll of antacids. He popped several in his mouth. Within seconds he clutched his chest.

At the same time, I had taken the microphone from Williams and announced, "Come on, everyone. Be your costume. Dance, laugh and kiss the person next to you. We're here to have fun."

In the far distance were the sounds of police sirens.

Reiner's face had turned ashen. He was having trouble breathing. He broke out into a cold sweat. One hand held the rifle, the other clutched at his chest. His breath became more rapid. He was panting for breath.

"Jesus Christ," Melendez shouted. "He's having a heart attack."

* * *

Evie had started crying. "Oh, God."
Everyone in the apartment had frozen, their eyes glued to the TV.
Abe said nothing, a smile on his face.

* * *

Reiner was struggling to sight through his scope. Everything was blurry. He saw many devils on the platform. His body started shaking. He blinked once, twice. He could no longer see. His body stiffened and with his last effort pulled the trigger.

The bullet hit the microphone. The sound was picked up by the sound equipment and resonated throughout the Bowl. People started screaming. Everyone started running hysterically.

Wrightson and his men, dressed as angels, mounted the stage and positioned themselves back to back. They pulled out their automatic weapons and started shouting, "Kill the Motherfuckers!"

At the same time Ali Akbar and his band of Islamic terrorists, dressed as Hassidim, stormed the stage. They pulled out their automatic weapons and started shouting, "Allah Akbar. " They shot at the angels, killing them all. The security teams, dressed as devils and Marie Antoinettes, pulled out their weapons and killed the Islamist/Hassidim.

An overhead police helicopter started firing tear gas into the Hollywood Bowl, and within minutes the bowl was filled with smoke.

* * *

A crowd had gathered around Abe and Evie, watching the live pictures from the Hollywood Bowl.

"Oh my God, Oh my God," Evie kept repeating.

"Yes, this time it's going to work out for both of us," Abe said to himself, a smile securely plastered on his face.

7 5

It took six days for the smoke to clear and on the seventh day, I was elected President of the United States in a landslide victory.

END

ACKNOWLEDGEMENTS

First of all, it goes without saying, but I am going to say it anyway. I am totally awed, inspired, love and loved by my beautiful wife, Renée Vollen, whose smile, love and cooking have natured and nurtured me. We have laughed and loved endlessly and will continue to do so.

Then there is the wonderful collection of human quanta that came together to produce this book.

It started in the dog park where Helen Sedwick pushed me to self-publish. She led me to Carla King, who became my Virgil leading me through the Hell and Purgatory of the mechanics of self-publishing. Carla, in turn, opened the gates of Paradise, sending me to Danielle Murdoch for a startling website, and Janna Lopez to create an ingenious marketing plan.

These are the fantastic women who flocked around me, carefully lifting me out of my safe nest and opened the world for me to fly in.

And, of course, photographer Lars Kampmann, who captured my mask of inherent intelligence, and Jim Shepard of Octagon Lab for the cover.

ABOUT THE AUTHOR

Eugene Shapiro is a seasoned satirical political novelist and screenwriter. His wit and intellect are results of majoring in political science in grad school, years of traveling the globe, serving in the 82nd Airborne during the Korean War, working for the U.S. state department in India, driving New York cabs, and importing Burgundy wine. Shapiro resides in Northern California with his wife, Renée, his two Mexican rescue dogs, and today battles metastatic prostate cancer. Resilience has proven for Shapiro that honesty and a sense of humor go a long way towards creating an adventurous life.

You can contact him at:

www.HowTheDevilBecamePresident.com
DavidSavage4President@hotmail.com